SPECIAL PLACES

BY THE AUTHOR

Fiction

BLACK WEATHER

THE LAST ENEMY

FERAL

FAGO

Nonfiction

SPECIAL PLACES: IN SEARCH OF SMALL TOWN AMERICA

THE MEDICAL DETECTIVES

THE RIVER WORLD AND OTHER EXPLORATIONS

THE ORANGE MAN

WHAT'S LEFT: REPORTS ON A DIMINISHING AMERICA

A MAN NAMED HOFFMAN

THE NEUTRAL SPIRIT

THE DELECTABLE MOUNTAINS

THE INCURABLE WOUND

ELEVEN BLUE MEN

Edited

CURIOSITIES OF MEDICINE

SPECIAL PLACES

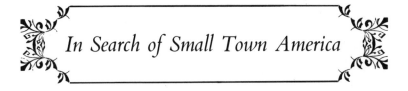

In Search of Small Town America

BERTON ROUECHÉ

with an introduction by William Shawn

Little, Brown and Company — Boston Toronto

FIRST EDITION

All the material in this book has previously appeared in *The New Yorker* in somewhat different form.

LIBRARY OF CONGRESS CATALOGING IN PUBLICATION DATA
Roueché, Berton, 1911-
Special places.
   Originally appeared in the New Yorker in a some-
what different form.
   Contents: Stapleton, Nebraska — Welch, West
Virginia — Hermann, Missouri — [etc.]
   1. City and town life — United States — Addresses,
essays, lectures.   2. United States — Social life
and customs — 1971-   — Addresses, essays,
lectures.   I. Title.
E169.02.R68   973'.09734   82-15256
ISBN 0-316-75935-2   AACR2

VB

Designed by Susan Windheim

*Published simultaneously in Canada
by Little, Brown & Company (Canada) Limited*

PRINTED IN THE UNITED STATES OF AMERICA

To my traveling companion

"I know no town like any other,
if it be truly known."
— MATTHEW FAIRE
(1841–1903)

Contents

Introduction

STAPLETON, Nebraska. Welch, West Virginia. Pella, Iowa. Corydon, Indiana. Hermann, Missouri. Crystal City, Texas. Hope, Arkansas. No town is ordinary, but there is one particular way in which all seven of these towns are extraordinary. They share the distinction of having been chosen by Berton Roueché as subjects for the series of remarkable portraits that make up this book. Roueché is best known, perhaps, for his tales of medical detection, but he is a writer with more than one enthusiasm. He has written a series of pieces about people who have devoted themselves passionately to various homely occupations, such as making chairs and growing potatoes. He has also written a number of suspense novels, and he has written about his travels. Finally, he has written about our country's small towns. Whatever he encounters he responds to acutely as an artist. Yet certainly his is the art that conceals art. His words are so plain, his sentences so chaste, his rhythms so natural that one can overlook the presence of the writer and see straight through to the matter at hand. His work is without ornamentation, without mannerism, without self-display — devoid of contrivance or sentimentality. He sees clearly and writes clearly, and sees only what is there. He is an inspired observer, but he makes no fuss about it. Like Roueché himself and all his towns, his writing is unhurried, quiet, peaceable, warm. I have been Roueché's editor for thirty-five years, and never once have I known him to act ungracefully. Having simplified his own life down to the essentials of family, friends, and work (with a blithe indifference to publicity, celebrity, and social glamour), he has developed a style that is notable for its simplicity, its purity. For these geographical portraits it turns out to be the right style. He gravitates toward precisely the details that catch the individual spirit of each town, and he sets them down with poetry and with respect.

Stapleton, Nebraska, is a town that has no crime and has never had a murder. It's the custom there to paint old teakettles and coffeepots, plant them with petunias and marigolds, and hang them from poles. In the coal-mining town of Welch, West Virginia, every view is closed by a mountain. Mayor William B. Swope lives in a big stone house. "My grandfather built this house in nineteen and three," Mayor Swope told Roueché. "Welch was just beginning then, and there were a lot of highly skilled stonemasons around. 'Tallies,' they called them. The retaining walls you see all over town, the Tallies built them all. Beautiful work. But a lost art now.... The Tallies built this house." Twenty-five years ago, a native son of Crystal City, Texas, named Ben Jackson wrote a memoir of the "epochal event of fifty years before." Jackson wrote, "When our artesian well came in, everybody in town gathered around it, and there before us was the most beautiful sight in the world. A great dome of water lifted of its own force and gushed to a crystal mound" — giving the town its name. It's mostly a Mexican-American town; chili is served on the motel's breakfast buffet. A history teacher at the Central High School in Corydon, Indiana, told Roueché, "Corydon's still on a human scale. There's a sense of the seasons. There's a closeness to the basics. It's something to be able to hear a rooster crow these days." Pella, Iowa, is a Dutch town, founded, planned, and built almost single-handedly by a pastor named Scholte, who was born in Amsterdam in 1805, and who wanted his town to "reject Holland but ardently retain everything Dutch," and this is what it has done: it is a town filled with delft and a kind of folk painting called Hindeloopen, a town that has a Tulip Festival and a Tulip Queen, and where the only Sunday-morning sound is the sound of church bells. Hope, Arkansas, another churchgoing town, is also a railroad town, which, according to Roueché, "sees — and hears — the daily passage of some forty freight trains." It calls itself the Watermelon Capital of the World. Hermann, Missouri, which was founded by Pennsylvania German-Americans in 1837 "for the purpose of establishing a settlement that would perpetuate German culture and the German language on the free American frontier," is still resolutely German in character and looks more or less as it did at the time of the Civil War. A few years ago, Van and Bessie Moore were driving through the country (they then lived in St. Louis) and crossed a bridge and found themselves in Hermann. Mrs. Moore said to her husband, "Here it is — I've finally made it home. Nothing but good can happen to us here." She was speaking not only for herself and for many other residents of Hermann but for a host of people living in all the seven towns Roueché has written about. He describes the houses, the taverns, the motels, the restaurants, the gas stations, the schools, the banks, the food stores, the liquor stores, the drugstores, the hardware stores — the Kwik Kar Wash, Larry's Bottle Shop, Bea's Golden Bull Restaurant, the Davidson Pool Room, Griffin's Dry Goods, the This Is It Gift Shop, the Casa de Lorenzo Motel — but, most important, he describes the people and how they live their lives from day to day. Few other towns can have been as accurately or affectionately defined as these. Roueché has given them an existence apart from the existence they already had. In the literature of place, they are immortal.

—WILLIAM SHAWN

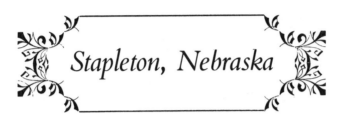

Stapleton, Nebraska

S TAPLETON, where I lived for a month, the month of May, is a crossroads county seat in the Sand Hills country of western Nebraska. It was founded in 1912, and it has a population of three hundred and three. The Sand Hills are grassy dunes. They are great, oceanic waves of sand with a carpeting of the rich native grass that nourished the buffalo — sand bluestem, prairie sand reed, sand lovegrass, switch grass, needle and thread. Briefly green in the short prairie spring, then brown and dry and blowing in the perpetual prairie wind, the Sand Hills form the largest natural cattle range in the United States. They cover all or much of twenty Nebraska counties. One of these, Cherry County, is bigger than Connecticut and Rhode Island combined. Logan County, of which Stapleton is the seat, is the smallest of the Sand Hills counties. It is roughly twice the size of Cape Cod. The Sand Hills grasslands are the quiddity of Stapleton. They surround and contain and sustain it. They also isolate it. Stapleton is the only town in Logan County. Its nearest neighbor is the village of Arnold (population 755), twenty miles away to the east, in Custer County. North Platte (population 19,287), the metropolis of western Nebraska, is twenty-nine miles to the south. Thedford (population 293) is thirty-six miles to the north, and a roadside hamlet called Tryon (population 166) is twenty-seven miles to the west.

There is nothing between Stapleton and its neighbors — nothing at all. No roadhouses, no driveins, not even a filling station. There is only the long, empty highway and the range. Sometimes, in the distance, one can see a clump of trees and a windmill and a ranch house. The population of rural Logan County — that is, the county exclusive of Stapleton — is six hundred and ninety-one.

Stapleton is linked to its neighbors by two highways. They are U.S. Highway 83, the main north-and-south route in the area, and Nebraska Highway 92, running east and west. Both are single-lane blacktop highways, and they intersect at a right-angle crossing about half a mile east of the village. Stapleton stands in a windbreak grove of cottonwoods and Chinese elms, and can be only glimpsed from the intersection. Except in winter, when the leaves are down, travelers often pass it unawares. Highway 92 runs through the middle of Stapleton and is one of its two main streets, but Stapleton is not a highway village. It was differently designed. It was laid out as a railroad town. Stapleton came into being (on a section — or square mile — of land provided by two pioneer cattlemen) as the terminus of a branch line of the Union Pacific Railroad, and its second main street is Main Street, which runs north and south. Main Street is eighty feet wide and half a mile long, and it runs from one end of town to the other. It begins at the yellow clapboard Union Pacific Depot, at the north end, and it ends at the red brick Stapleton Consolidated School. There is a parade on Main Street every weekday morning (weather permitting) during the school year. This is part of the training of the Stapleton High School Band. The band marches — flags flying and drum majorettes strutting — out from the school and up to the depot and back. People come out of the Main Street stores and offices and stand and watch it go by.

Stapleton has always been a village. It has never been much larger than it is today. Once, around 1930, its population climbed as high as five hundred and one. The village is now a little smaller than it was at the time of the First World War. But Stapleton has the look of a town — an urban look. There are no wandering, cowpath streets, no straggle out along the highway. It is plotted in the urban gridiron pattern, and its limits are clearly defined. The backyards of the outermost houses all end at a barbed-wire fence, and beyond the fence is the range. Stapleton has several urban amenities. It has a municipal park with a tennis court and picnic ovens and picnic tables and benches. It maintains the county ambulance (the nearest hospitals are St. Mary's Hospital and Memorial Hospital, in North Platte), and the drivers, members of the fire department, are trained in first aid. It has a municipal waterworks and a municipal sewer system. Its telephone system is fully automatic, and the lines are laid underground. Most of the streets are lighted and paved, and the paved streets all have sidewalks. The streets are named in the functional urban fashion. The north-south streets — the streets that parallel Main Street — are named for the letters of the alphabet. There are ten of these streets — A Street through J Street. (Main Street runs between F and G.) The other streets are numbered. They run from First Street, at the depot, to Sixth Street, at the school. Highway 92 is known formally as Third Street. There are, however, no street signs in Stapleton, and (except for Main Street) the street names are never used. The intersection of Main Street and Highway 92 is usually called the Corner.

Most Stapletonians are born in a North Platte hospital, and almost all of them are buried in one or another of three Logan County cemeteries — McCain, St. John's, and Loup Valley. Loup Valley Cemetery is the smallest and the most remote. It lies in a fold in the range about ten miles west of Stapleton, on the road to Tryon. St. John's, a Roman Catholic cemetery that was consecrated in 1915, and McCain are both just east of town, on the road that leads to Arnold. McCain is the largest of the three cemeteries, and by far the oldest. It was established (as the gift of the widow of a pioneer named Robert McCain) in 1884, and it occupies four acres on a hilltop planted with bushy box elders and big, spreading cedars. It offers a commanding view of the surrounding countryside, and also of the past. A majority of the early settlers (and the founders of the established local families) are buried there: Miller, Burnside, Hartzell, Clark, Wheeler, Smith, Wells, Bay, Perry, Erickson, Abrams, Joedeman, Salisbury, Loudon. Many of the pioneers were veterans of the Civil War, all having served with the Union Army. The notations on their headstones are geographically descriptive: "Co. C, 9 Ohio Cavalry"; "Co. A, 81 Pa. Infantry"; "Co. H, 71 N. Y. Infantry"; "10 Indiana Cav."; "Co. F, 86 Ill. Inf."; "Co. D, 1st Iowa Cavalry"; "Co. E, 5th Iowa Infantry." Except for an elaborate white marble shaft commemorating Robert McCain, and one or two other monumental monuments, the headstones are modest tablets. A few are inscribed with conventional pieties ("Though thou art done, fond mem'ry clings to thee"), but most of them carry only a name and a date. The given names of the men are equally conventional: Joseph, William, Richard, John, Edward. The given names of the women at McCain, and also at Loup Valley (though not, of course, at St. John's), are more imaginative. Some of them are wildly so: Melita, Alvirda, Glenola, Vernie Lynn, Tressa, Verla, Idara, Delma, Velna, Zetta, Uhleen, Berdie, Zella, Lesta, Verga, Lenna, Jacobina, Dalorus, Tilitha, Caline, Mayden, Sedona, Orpha, Doralie, Urah. These names are not, as I at first supposed, the fancies of a vanished generation. Such names are still popular in Stapleton.

A high-school senior I met is named Vaneta. One of her class-
mates is named Wilda. A first grader, about whom I read, is
named Jeanna. A second grader is named Tena. There is a sixth
grader named Kerri. And the first name of Mrs. Robert
A. Perry, the wife of a prominent Logan County rancher, is
Alta May.

✦

Practically everybody in Stapleton lives on the south side of
town. There are only five families on the north side of the
highway. The churches — Presbyterian, Catholic, and Assembly
of God — are all in the residential area. The First Presbyterian Church — the largest and oldest of the Stapleton churches
— and the fundamentalist Assembly of God are both on Main
Street, south of the Corner, and St. John's Catholic Church is a
block to the west. There is plenty of space in Stapleton (there
are vacant lots on every block), but most of the houses are built
on fifty-foot plots. "The Sand Hills is a big country," James
Morey, a farmer who now lives in town, told me. "If you ever
homesteaded up on the Dismal River, like I did, you'd know
what I'm talking about. People like company. They like to have
close neighbors." Some of the houses are brick, some are asbestos
shingle, and some are clapboard painted white, but they are
otherwise much alike. The usual house has one story, with a
little stepped stoop and a low-pitched pyramidal roof. The
chairman of the Board of Trustees, the governing body of
Stapleton — a retired (and reputedly well-to-do) merchant and
landowner named John Beckius — lives in such a house, and so
does Mrs. Vivian Nelson, a laundress. The biggest house in town
is the Catholic rectory. Most of the houses have flower and
vegetable gardens, and the lawns are often strangely orna-
mented. Some people move old, axe-handled backyard pumps
around to the front and paint them in bright colors. Many

people cut openings in plastic Clorox bottles and hang them up as houses for purple martins. People also paint old coffeepots and teakettles and hang them in groups from poles and plant them with geraniums and petunias and marigolds. The garage of one house has a garden of cabbage-size pink roses and giant blue delphiniums painted on an outside wall. "That wall goes back to our painting fad," Mrs. Earl Glandon, an amateur artist and the wife of a former postmaster, told me. "A professional artist came to town for a while and gave painting lessons, and there were about fourteen ladies that joined the class. One of the ladies painted that garage wall. Another lady, a widow lady, heard about a famous old sod house out south of town somewhere, and she went there and painted a picture of it, and a little later the man who owned the sod house asked her about the picture, and she invited him over to see it, and he came and they got friendly and he married her. He moved her into his sod house, and the first thing she did was to paint it. She painted wisteria around the door and morning glories climbing up the walls of the house. It was like that garage. She made it look more cheerful."

The main business block in Stapleton is Main Street just north of the Corner. It is a sun-baked block in summer — the only block in Stapleton without a twilit canopy of trees — but the sidewalks in front of some of the buildings are shaded by metal awnings. Most of the buildings on the block are one-story buildings of red or yellow brick. About half of them have high false fronts. There are two vacant buildings on the block. One is an old store full of broken fixtures. The other is a boarded-up movie house. It went out of business in 1955, but there is a painted-over name still visible on the façade: "The New Theater." The block contains six stores. Three of them are grocery stores (Black's Thriftway Grocery, Denny's Market, and

Ewoldt's Grocery & Locker), and there is a hardware store (Hanna's Supply), a feed store (Miller Ranch Supply), and a farm-equipment store (Salisbury Implement Company). All of them are more or less general stores. Ewoldt's is almost a department store. It occupies three rooms on the ground floor of a two-story building that was once the Hildenbrandt Hotel (there are twenty-one numbered rooms, including a bridal suite, on the second floor), and it sells — along with meats and groceries — drugs, cosmetics, notions, toys, memorial wreaths, school supplies, work clothes, boots, big hats, and ice. The other business buildings on the block are a laundromat (Bud's Holiday Laundry), a bowling alley (Bronco Bowl), the Stapleton *Enterprise* (a weekly paper), and the Bank of Stapleton. There is also a two-story (with a false front) Masonic Temple, and an American Legion Post. The bank is on the northwest corner of the Corner, and it is the most imposing building on the block. It is a square brick building with ornamental cornices and glass-brick windows and a high, pedimented roof. Along the highway side is a two-rail iron-pipe railing. On Saturday afternoons, there are usually a couple of cowboys sitting there with their heels hooked over the bottom rail and their hats tipped down on their noses.

The Stapleton Post Office, a red brick building that somewhat resembles the bank, is on the southwest corner of the Corner. Across Main Street from the post office is Chesley's Barber Shop. "I've only got one complaint," Everette C. Chesley, the barber, told me. "It isn't about long hair. The kids around here don't wear their hair what I would call short, but they do come in and get haircuts. My complaint is shaves. I used to shave maybe fifteen fellows of a Saturday. The last time I shaved a fellow was an old man two months ago. I might as well get rid of my razors. A razor is like an arm or a leg. It goes

dead unless you use it." Next door to the barbershop is the
Logan County Courthouse. The courthouse was built in 1963
and is the newest building in Stapleton. It is an L-shaped
building faced with polished pink granite, with a flagpole in
front and a parking lot and an acre of well-kept lawn. There is
a little cluster of businesses up around the depot. The office and
storage bins of the Stapleton Mill & Elevator Co. are there, and
a feed lot, and two lumberyards — the S. A. Foster Lumber
Company and the Greenslit Lumber Company. Their yards are
stacked with big round metal water troughs and creosoted fence
posts and spools of barbed wire. (In Stapleton, as everywhere
else west of Pittsburgh, barbed wire is "bob wire.") Except for
two living-room beauty parlors — one (Dotti's Beauty Salon)
on the west side of town and the other (Beauty Shop) in a
house near the school — the other Stapleton businesses are all
situated on the highway. Just west of the Corner are a beer bar
and liquor store (Wagon Wheel Tavern) and a Rural Elec-
trification Administration garage. East of the Corner are a
farm-equipment store (Magnuson Implement Company), two
filling stations (East Side Skelly Service and A. A. Gulf Service),
the fire station, and the Whiteway Cafe & Motel.

"My wife and I took over the newspaper in nineteen sixty,"
Arthur French, the publisher of the *Enterprise*, told me. "We
came over from Tryon. Tryon is pretty little, and it's also pretty
staid. Stapleton is more like a town. When we first arrived here,
there were maybe a few more business places than there are
now. There was another cafe and a drugstore. But they were
mostly run by older people with their money down deep in
their pockets. They were just setting there. Now all the stores
have younger people in charge. Dick Black at the Thriftway
and Elwin Miller at the Ranch Supply and Dick Kramer at the
Skelly station, they're just in their twenties, and Alfred Ewoldt

isn't very much older. Neither is Dean Hanna, at the Gulf station. I'm still under forty myself. Even Ed Burnham — Edwin H. Burnham, the president of the bank and I guess you could say our leading citizen. He has the insurance agency there at the bank and he owns a lot of property and he has a big interest in the elevator and he's building himself a new fifty-thousand-dollar home out east of town. Even Ed is only about fifty. Ed believes in Stapleton, and he'll put up money to prove it. Ed gave me my start here with a very generous loan. We've also got a real nice Chamber of Commerce, with thirty-five members, and I think we've got a future. Our only problem is getting help. I could use another man in our printshop, and I had a fellow lined up down in the Platte. He drove up with his wife one day. They made a couple of passes around town and then came into the shop and the wife said, 'I didn't see the shopping center. Where is it?' I said we didn't have a shopping center here. 'Let's go,' she said."

The name of Edwin H. Burnham is often heard in Stapleton. He is not always in residence there (during my stay he was sojourning at a hunting lodge he has in Canada), but his presence is constantly felt. "Our banker is the pleasantest man you ever saw," Charles V. Greenslit, the owner of the lumberyard that bears his name, told me. "Hail fellow well met. Always smiling. Generous. Gave our village an ambulance. Gives to all the churches. Our old banker — the man who brought Ed Burnham here — he was just the opposite. He was conservative. He was the kind of banker who wouldn't think of making a loan unless you hardly needed the money. Burnham's happy to help anybody. And he's done well for himself. Real well. Everything he touches turns to money. I sometimes wonder how he does it. He's never here. But he's building himself a sixty-thousand-dollar home out east of town. So maybe he's planning to settle down." Everybody seems to think well of Burnham. "Ed Burnham is a real asset," Leslie M. Bay, the county judge, told me. "When we were getting ready to build the new courthouse, he got us a big bond break. He bid our building bonds down to three per cent, and then stepped back and let somebody else bid them in at two point eighty-five percent. One of our problems here is housing. Ed won't let a house fall down. He'll fix it up and put it back to work. He's always finding an old house out in the county somewhere and moving it into town. Right now, he's building himself a nice new home on some land he owns out east of here. I understand it's costing him in the neighborhood of seventy-five thousand dollars. Of course, Ed has improved himself. He's made a lot of money. But you'd never know he had a dime. He's as common as an old shoe. He'd just as soon set down and drink a bottle of beer as not. Wherever he's at, that's what he is. Ed's at home anywhere. He's a rancher out at your ranch. In Rome, he's a Roman."

✦

The Whiteway was my home in Stapleton. I had a room (with a big springy bed and a rocking chair and a table) in the Motel, and I took my meals at the Cafe. The Cafe occupies the front end of a long, narrow, shingle-sided building with a low, overhanging roof all around and a gravelly unpaved parking lot on three sides. The Motel is in back, behind the kitchen, and overlooks a chicken yard patrolled by three excitable roosters. It consists of five rooms (with baths) and the apartment of the manager. The Whiteway is owned by a woman in Hooker County, and it is leased from her by a Logan County farmer named James Wonch. (Wonch is a powerful man with a sha-ven head and dark-brown eyes. I had been in Stapleton about a week before I met him, and I was strangely struck by his appearance. There was something unusual about his looks that I couldn't quite identify. I thought at first that it must be his shaven head — and then I realized. The unusual thing was his eyes. Almost everybody in Stapleton — everybody but Wonch and one or two others — has blue eyes.) The manager of the Whiteway is a plump, pretty, white-haired widow (with blue eyes) named Clarice Olson, and she also does most of the cooking and all of the baking at the Cafe. "I open up at about six-thirty, and we close at night when the last customer gets up and leaves," Mrs. Olson told me. "That's usually around ten o'clock. Our people come in for breakfast, for second breakfast, for midmorning coffee, for noon dinner, for afternoon coffee, for supper, and for evening coffee. There's usually somebody waiting when I open up in the morning. Most of the time, it's Red Black. Red and his wife both work for the county. He's a road grader, and she cleans at the courthouse. Red drives her to work and them comes around for his coffee. Half the time, he opens the door for me. Then he sits and watches me get my baking started. I bake two dozen cinnamon rolls every morning, and about a half a dozen pies. Always apple, always cherry, and either lemon or chocolate meringue. Sometimes I make a few doughnuts. Then I get dinner started. My first dinner customer is Vera Gragg, one of the tellers at the bank. She comes in at eleven-thirty, on the dot. They're my most regular custom-ers — Vera and Red Black." Mrs. Olson's daughter, a divorcée named LaDonna Wisdom, is the regular Cafe waitress, and a young girl named Grace Young helps out when needed. For much of my stay, I was the only traveler at the Motel, but the Cafe was almost always crowded. There were always a couple of cars pulled up in front (nobody in Stapleton ever walks anywhere), and usually a dusty pickup truck from one of the farms or ranches. The Cafe is the social center of Stapleton. Almost everybody in town drops in at some time almost every

day. One Sunday afternoon, I counted a dozen cars parked
there. Three of them were Cadillacs.

The Cafe is a clean and comfortable cafe. It is warm in cold
weather and icily air-conditioned in summer, and the three outer
walls are windows. There are six cream-and-gold Formica
tables around the window walls, and a counter with five stools
across the back. A door at one end of the counter opens into a
private dining room that will accommodate about twenty
diners. The Chamber of Commerce holds its monthly dinner
meetings there. There is a soda fountain behind the counter
(with a display of candy bars and chewing gum and foil-
wrapped bandoliers of Alka-Seltzer), but the cooking is all done
in the kitchen. There is a jukebox the size of an organ near the
dining-room door, with an automated repertoire of "Lonesome
Highway" and "Sugar Shack" and a hundred other country-
and-Western tunes. There is a Coca-Cola machine and a Dr
Pepper machine and a cigarette machine. There is a bulletin
board on the wall near the jukebox with a calendar ("Com-
pliments Central Nebraska Commission Co., Broken Bow,
Nebr., Cattle Sale Every Saturday") and an assortment of bul-
letins ("Wanted: Write-in-Votes for Joe Klosen"; "Midwest
Breeders Cooperative: Beef & Dairy Semen, Liquid Nitrogen,
A-I Supplies"; "The Last Pages — for booking, call Steve Myers,
Bill Dolan, Doug Wallace, N. Platte"; "Bull Sale, Ogallala Sale
Barn, Ogallala, Nebr.: 39 Angus, 2 Charolais, 45 Herefords, 5
Shorthorns") and a motto ("No Man Is Good Enough to
Govern Another Without the Other's Consent"). There is a
blackboard menu on the wall behind the counter with one
permanent entry: "Roast Beef, $1.40." Other entries that appear
on the board from time to time are "Scalloped Potatoes & Ham,
$1.25" and "Salmon Loaf, $1.25." The roast beef is pot roast.
Steak is never listed on the menu but it is always available, and

it is always cut thin and always chicken-fried. There is a sign near the blackboard: "Margarine Served Here." The bread is Rainbo Bread.

One rainy morning, I lingered over breakfast at the Cafe. I sat at a window table and ate fried eggs and thick pancakes and watched the cars pull in and out and the customers come and go. Several of the cars had little decal American flags on the windows, and one had a bumper sticker: "Trust in Christ." Some sparrows were nesting under the eaves of the Cafe, and they flew from car to car, feeding on the insects shattered on the radiator grilles. I knew some of the customers by name and most of the others by sight. There were three R.E.A. technicians in cowboy hats and boots. There was Alfred Ewoldt in cowboy boots and a hunting cap. There was a young cowboy in a sweatshirt with lettering across the back: ". . . and a Follower of Women." There was an elderly farmer in bib overalls matching double or nothing for coffee with the waitress, LaDonna Wisdom. There was the county judge, Judge Bay, with a lump of snuff under his lower lip, and Mrs. Thomas Mahoney, the village clerk and the wife of a Union Pacific conductor. There were two school-bus drivers (of a total of nine) — Mrs. Beverly Lehmkuhler, a widow, and Mrs. Norman Yardley, the wife of the high-school principal — eating a second breakfast; they rise early to circle the county and bring the students in to school. There was Mrs. Noma Wells, the widow of a merchant and landowner, who spends much of her time driving around town in a saffron-yellow Cadillac. (Her car is one of five Cadillacs in Stapleton, and there are also three new Lincoln Continentals.) There was a thin girl in jeans and a T-shirt. There was James Wonch. There was a tall, stooped, flat-bellied cowboy in a rodeo shirt with the sleeves cut off at the shoulders. There was James Morey, the former Dismal River homesteader, with an old black hat on the back of his head, talking to the other waitress, Grace Young. I sat and looked and listened.

✦

James Morey: How about you and me having a date sometime?

Grace Young: I don't go out with old whiskery men.

James Morey: I could shave. But have I got a chance? I ain't going to shave in the middle of the week unless there's at least a chance.

✦

Mrs. Lehmkuhler: The first one I picked up this morning brought me an apple. And another one gave me some fudge. They're going to get me fat.

James Wonch: It's a funny thing. My dad used to walk to school. I rode a horse. But all my kids have to do is stand and wait for the bus.

✦

LaDonna Wisdom: One week, I cut down eating and I gained five pounds. When I stepped on the scales, I was real disgusted. So I went back to eating.

Elderly Farmer: I'll match you for one of them rolls.

✦

R.E.A. Man: Marijuana?

Second R.E.A. Man: They call it pot. It looks like it's moving this way. They say the kids have got it at Broken Bow.

Third R.E.A. Man: We used to call it Mary Jane.

✦

Mrs. Mahoney: I don't know about the Platte. But they've never had to draft a boy from here. Or from Tryon. Or from Arnold, for that matter.

✦

Girl in the T-Shirt: No, I've just got the two. But I was

married at fifteen and I'm only eighteen now and I'm not going to have no more. For a while, anyway. I will say this. I never had no trouble having any of my kids. The girl next to me the last time, she had a Cesarean. My second baby, he's ten months now, but a couple of months ago he couldn't sit up or anything. He had the rickets. They started giving him lots of vitamins, and now he can sit and everything real good.

✦

Mrs. Wells: I'm washing at Bud's this morning, so while I'm working I thought I'd have some coffee.

✦

Mrs. Mahoney: LaDonna, I came away this morning without any matches. Have you got some?

LaDonna Wisdom: Here — can you catch?

Mrs. Mahoney: I catch real good. When you've got a boy in the Boy Scouts working on merit badges, you can do a lot of things. I can tie knots and make a fire and talk in the Morse code. I can do a hundred things I never wanted to do.

Mrs. Yardley: Be glad you haven't got a daughter. Mine has been practicing for the 4-H cake demonstration, and she ended up in the kitchen last Saturday with eighteen sponge cakes.

✦

Judge Bay: It don't blow every day, but then it blows twice the next day to make up for it.

✦

Mrs. Mahoney: . . . sewing on Sunday. My mother would have said that I'll never get to Heaven until I stop and take those stitches out with my nose. She also used to say that you haven't learned to sew until you've learned to rip.

✦

The cowboy in the sleeveless shirt got up to go, and stopped and looked at me, and then came over. "Excuse me," he said.

"But you look mighty familiar to me. I wonder haven't I seen you someplace before. Where are you from?"

I told him that I lived in New York.

"That could be it," he said. "I could have seen you there. I used to travel — before and after the service. My feet have been on every soil in the continental United States and the world. Except only Russia. I used to speak fourteen different languages, but I didn't keep it up. Now I've only got but one. Well, *choco-chuco-mungo-mango-boola-mack.*"

"What?" I said.

"That's Indian for 'See you later,' " he said.

I was ready to leave, too. I pushed back my chair and put a tip on the table ("You don't have to do that every time," LaDonna said), and paid my bill, and followed the cowboy out. My breakfast, including orange juice and coffee, cost sixty cents.

✦

The Cafe is not exclusively an adult gathering place. It also serves as the corner drugstore for the teenage boys of Stapleton. There are a few boys hanging around nearly every evening, but their big night there is Friday night. They drift up after supper in their dress-up clothes — clean, faded bluejeans, two-toned, high-heeled boots with fancy stitching, big hats (felt in winter, straw in summer), and brightly patterned shirts with double pockets and snaps for buttons. Most of the boys have cars (drivers are licensed at sixteen in Nebraska), and they lean against the parked cars in front of the Cafe and kick gravel and wrestle and yell to each other ("Hey Larry — where's Kramer and those guys?") and stomp inside and play the jukebox and get Cokes and come shoving out and trade arm punches, and the boys with dates drive up and the others flock around and make jokes ("Hey, is that a new shirt, or is that a new shirt?"), and the girls in the cars laugh and comb their hair and shriek back and forth, and every now and then a car with a couple in it will start up abruptly ("Watch him lay some rubber now. He's put fifty thousand miles on those tires and half of it is just in starts") and take off down the highway and after a while come roaring back and park again and sit and then suddenly charge off once more, with the radio thumping and twanging, and this time the car will head out toward U.S. 83 and Arnold, or west toward Tryon, and pretty soon all the couples are gone and the jukebox stops and the Cafe lights go out, and then the car doors begin to slam and the engines race and the remaining cars move off and up to the depot and down past the school and home.

✦

The courthouse is the office building of Stapleton. It houses around a dozen village, county, state, and federal offices. The village clerk and the village marshal; the county clerk, the county treasurer, the county (or probate) judge, the county welfare director, the county Board of Commissioners (executive body concerned with taxes, roads, budgets, assessments), and the county sheriff; the state Agricultural Extension Service representative (or county agent); and two agencies of the United States Department of Agriculture — all have offices there. The building also houses a courtroom (with jury room and chambers for the visiting district judge at his quarterly sessions), a jail (with two cells), a local-history museum, and a public library.

The museum is an accretion of odds and ends (a wooden lemon press, an 1807 edition of the Bible, two shaving mugs, a pair of "Driving Gloves worn by E. R. Smith when he drove the second car in Logan County in 1907," a blue glass ball stamped "Harden's Hand Grenade Fire Extinguisher Pat. 1871") arranged in a case in the courtroom foyer, but the library is a substantial one. It has an annual budget for books of five hundred dollars, and an accessible collection of some thirty-four thousand books, including a shelf of standard Nebraska authors — Willa Cather, Mari Sandoz, John G. Neihardt, Bess Streeter Aldrich. It is an active library, and the children are introduced to it at an early age through a weekly story hour conducted by volunteer readers. Some women drive in with their children from distant ranches for the weekly reading. ("This is a real conservative community," Charles Hunnel, the superintendent of the Stapleton school, told me. "The people here believe very highly in education. Our annual budget at the school is over two hundred thousand dollars. That's almost half the total tax income of the county. We have a very high educational level. More than half of our high-school graduates go on to college, and we have practically no dropouts. In my seven years in this job, we've had just two — two girls dropped out to get married. We haven't produced any geniuses. It isn't an intellectual community. But there's a real respect for learning.") The librarian is a widow named Florence L. Brown. Mrs. Brown is also something of a local historian. "People are always asking me where Stapleton got its name," she told me. "Well, I finally found out. I found an editorial in a copy of the *Enterprise* for October 17, 1912, that explained everything. I made a copy for the library, and here it is. Sit down and read it." It read:

Mr. D. C. Stapleton has for the past thirty years felt an abiding interest and faith in the future of central western Nebraska, and while his larger interests have called him abroad for the greater part of the time, for several years past, he has never lost sight of the fact that out here in Nebraska was the place of all the rest that he could call "home," for it was here he homesteaded in the year 1884 and it was in recognition of his high ideals of

what western Nebraska ought to be and do, and his constant
efforts toward that goal that this city was named "Stapleton" in
his honor.

There is no crime in Stapleton. People leave the keys in their
cars and the doors of their houses unlocked. Don Vetter, the
village marshal, wears a policeman's blue cap, but he is only
nominally a peace officer. His main job is operating the water
plant, the sewage plant, and the village dump. Law and order is
formally represented in Stapleton by the Logan County sheriff.
The sheriff is a big, comfortable man of sixty-two with a star on
his shirt and a smile on his face and a revolver in a drawer of his
desk. His name is Arthur Wiley, and he has been sheriff since
1954. "Order is no problem here," he told me. "This is a peaceable town. Nobody crowds anybody. There's plenty of leeway.
A man has got the freedom to go out and holler if he wants to.
Law is what I'm mostly concerned with. I mean summonses
and traffic offenses and things like that. No local boy has ever
got in serious trouble in my time in office. Once in a while, I
break up a fight at the bar. That's usually in August, when we
have our fair and rodeo and some cowboy pours a glass of beer
down some other guy's neck. We've never in history had a
murder here. I did get shot up once. A couple of kids started out
at Imperial — down south of Ogallala — breaking into places
and stealing what they wanted. This was in 1961, in the win-
tertime, with snow on the ground. Well, they came into town
here one night and broke into Ewoldt's store. Ewoldt lives
upstairs, but they didn't know that, and he heard them messing
around and called me at home, and I came driving up and
caught them up by the depot. They were in their sock feet,
trying on a bunch of cowboy boots they'd stole. Their car was
full of fancy shirts and Stetson hats and forty-dollar boots — all

kinds of cowboy stuff. I got them out of their car and had the driver standing with his hands on the roof in the regular way, and I was frisking him. Well, all of a sudden the other boy came around the car, and when I looked up he had a revolver in his hand. I slipped behind the driver. My gun was an old .351 automatic — what they call a riot gun. I told the boy to drop that revolver. But the driver gave a jump and pushed up my gun, and before I could get it back in position the other boy fired his revolver. I don't know how he missed me, but he did. He hit the driver instead — hit him in the arm. My gun was ready then, and I fired and hit him at the belt, on the buckle, and staggered him against the car. I told him to drop his gun. But he didn't. He up and shot me. Shot me in the left side, and the bullet went through both lobes of my liver. All I felt was like a hot poker or something touching me there. But I dropped my gun and sat down in a snowdrift. The boys jumped back in their car and made to drive off. But before they more than got started I reached around and found my gun and fired and shot out their front tire. The driver jumped out yelling and put his hand up — his good hand. But the other one, he was still acting up. He called me a dirty s.o.b. and a lot worse, and started shooting at me again. So I did the same. He was leaning over the top of the car, and my first shot only hit the shoulder padding on his coat. Then I shot into the car and blew out the windows in his face. He couldn't see with all that glass flying, but I didn't feel like shooting anymore, and Don Vetter came running up, and that was it. They hauled the three of us off to the hospital at North Platte to get patched up. I was laid up there for quite a few weeks. One of the boys turned out to be fourteen years old, and the other one was fifteen. They both got something like eighteen months of correction. The boy that did all the shooting, he came out and turned into a pretty solid citizen. I understand he's never given anybody any more trouble. But the other boy — I don't know. I never heard."

♦

The principal business of the courthouse is the farms and ranches of Logan County. Their needs and responsibilities make up most of the routine work of the county clerk and the county treasurer and the county judge and the county commissioners, and they are the entire concern of the county agent and the two Department of Agriculture agencies. The Logan county agent is also the county agent of McPherson County, the neighboring county on the west. This gives him a district almost the size of Delaware. He is a crewcut young man with a faraway look, named Edmond A. Cook. "This is conservative country," he told me. "There are progressive people — people who adapt to the modern world — but the other kind are still around. 'Conservative' isn't really the right word. The people I mean are rigid. They're self-sufficient and individualistic. They still have the pioneer mentality. Their grandfathers *were* the pioneers out here. Well, a county agent is an educator. My job is to take the research information from the experimental stations and get it to the farmers in a form they can use. This means meetings and workshops, and the subjects are insect problems, crops — feed crops — and irrigation. We've got an interesting project going on now. It's a new way of growing corn in this dry country. Sod corn, we call it. There's no tillage — you plant rows of corn in the untouched sod. The growth of the grass is retarded chemically for about thirty days. That gives the corn a head start. Then the grass comes along in the normal way and holds the soil between the rows, and after the corn is harvested the grass is there for fall pasture and cover through the winter. The sod is precious here. The wind is the enemy. We have plenty of water, but it's all underground. There's an ocean of pure water, the

sweetest in the world, under these Sand Hills. The trouble is we
get only about eighteen inches of rain a year — about half of
what you get back East — and the wind blows all the time. The
sod is the only thing that keeps the land from blowing away.
We almost lost it back in the thirties, you know. I don't know
how our sod-corn project will work out. There are people who
will give it serious attention. But there are also those who
won't. They're still back there with the homesteaders who
wouldn't change — who kept on plowing the dust and over-
grazing the range. Nobody can tell them anything. They have
to be in pretty bad trouble before they'll come to me for help."

The U.S.D.A. agencies that have offices in the courthouse are
the Agricultural Stabilization and Conservation Service and the
Soil Conservation Service. Each consists of a manager and a
couple of women clerks. The Agricultural Stabilization and
Conservation Service administers the federal crop-control (or
production-adjustment) program, and it has been represented
in Stapleton since 1959 by a native of Tryon (and a former
rancher and Army officer) named William Griffith. "I'm a
native and I'm prejudiced," he told me, "but I've observed a
good many other places, and the Sand Hills country is hard to
beat for good living. You can buy a half of beef that you've
selected yourself, and Ewoldt's will butcher it and age it and
keep it for you in their locker. Or a lamb or a hog. There's good
pheasant shooting and good deer hunting — did you ever taste
venison salami? The people are friendly. Maybe they're too
friendly — everybody knows everybody's business. We have
very little changeover. People come here and they don't want to
leave. Our teachers stay on forever. We have only one serious
problem. It's the economic problem that's threatening all of
rural and small-town America. We can't keep our young people. The farms and ranches are getting bigger and bigger and

more and more mechanized, and the jobs are getting fewer and fewer. Not many of our local boys can hope to make a living here. They want to stay, but they can't — not unless they make a special effort. My youngest son is at the University of Nebraska, and his plan is to be a veterinarian so he can stay on here in the Sand Hills. Randy Joe Kramer, the salutatorian of the senior class at the high school this year, is another example. He's going to the university to study agriculture. He wants to be a county agent. On the other hand, there are John Beckius's two sons. They're more typical. There wasn't anything for them here. One of them is working down at the Platte, and the other is out in Denver."

The manager of the Soil Conservation Service office is a broad, smiling, bespectacled man (with brown eyes) named John H. Sautter. Sautter is a former high-school teacher and an authority on the pasture grasses of western Nebraska, and his job is counseling the ranchers of Logan and McPherson Counties on how to preserve and improve their range. The experience has given him a view of human nature much like that of the county agent, Cook. "The better the rancher, the more apt he is to ask us for help," he told me. "The poor ones don't bother. It's like everything else — the less you know, the less you want to know." I spent an afternoon out in the field with Sautter. He had been asked by a prosperous rancher to draft an improvement program for some grassland a few miles north of town, and we drove out there together in a government pickup truck that was geared to riding the range.

It was a beautiful afternoon, with a high, blue sky and a horizon of great white clouds and a cooling flow of breeze. There was a meadowlark on almost every fencepost, and a ring of old automobile tires laid flat around the foot of every telephone pole. The meadowlark is the state bird of Nebraska, and it has the distinction, now rare among state birds (how often does one see a bluebird in New York?), of being ubiquitous in its state. The tires are a protective contrivance peculiar to the Sand Hills. "Cattle are one of the problems of a cattle range," Sautter told me. "Cattle like to scratch themselves, and they particularly like to scratch against a pole where they can circle around and around. Those tires keep them back and away. They don't like the feel of them underfoot. Otherwise, they'd go scratching around until they dug a trench in the ground and the pole got loose and fell out. Their trails are almost as bad. Cattle are great creatures of habit. They'll follow the same little track through a gap in the hills until they've dug a trench, and with the kind of wind we have out here it doesn't take long for a trench to grow into a gully."

We turned off the highway at an opening in the fence and went over a gridiron cattle guard. We headed across a range hub-deep in grass. There were cattle grazing on a slope in the distance, and off to the right was the long green wall of a windbreak. "This country was practically treeless in the In-dian-and-buffalo days," Sautter told me. "The only trees were along the Platte and the Dismal River, up north, and some of the little creeks. The windbreaks are all man-made. The early settlers planted them with trees they hauled all the way up from the river bottoms. That's why you see so many cottonwoods. A cottonwood will grow from a slip, like a willow. Windbreaks are part of my job. A lot of the big ones around here were put in back in the thirties. Some of them are a mile long. Shelter belts, they called them then. Those were desperate years. People had the idea that trees would increase the humidity. It was a sur-vival of the kind of wishful thinking that told the first settlers that rain followed the plow. In the thirties, they thought trees would bring rain. They thought they would break the drought.

The design of a windbreak depends on the site, and also on what it's specifically for — to shelter your house or your livestock, or to protect a field or an orchard or a garden. We think a windbreak should be at least four rows deep. Five is better. The conventional design puts tall, broad-leaf trees, like ash or Chinese elm, in the middle and smaller, denser evergreens, like pines and cedars, in the outer rows. My own preference is for exclusively pine and cedar. That windbreak over there is one of the older ones. It's a mixture of various plantings — box elder, Chinese elm, Russian olive, cottonwood, cedar, and even some wild plum. And if you'll look up there — off near the end — do you see something moving? That's a little herd of antelope."

We bumped slowly on across the range. The range was not entirely grass. There were occasional scatterings of wild flowers — blue pentstemon, yellow wild mustard, orange gromwell. We cut around the side of a hill and labored up an easier slope and came out on a windy plateau. The range spread out below us. A tiny car crept along the faraway highway. Sautter stopped the truck and rolled down his window. "This is excellent range," he said. "It's in good condition, too. Predominantly sand bluestem. That little shrublike plant you see here and there is a legume we call leadplant. When you see it growing undisturbed like that, it's an indication of good range condition. It means the cattle have plenty of other things to eat. They'll eat leadplant, but generally not until they've grazed off the best of the grass. It's a different story down there in the valley. This is natural range up here. The valley has been farmed, and the native grasses are just about gone. What you see there is panic grass and six-week fescue and western ragweed. And a little buffalo grass. You probably can't see the buffalo grass. It's real short — never gets higher than four or five inches. I happen to know it's there. People are always talking and writing about buffalo grass. I guess it sounds romantic. Buffalo grass is a native grass, but that doesn't make it desirable. It probably came in wherever the buffalo overgrazed the range. It has one good use. It's tough and will stand a lot of traffic. We use it around here in the outfield in the ballparks. It's going to take work to bring that valley back. The homesteaders did just about everything they could to ruin this land. They never learned to understand it. They grew a lot of corn because corn was what they knew. That bared the soil at planting time in the spring, and then in the fall they turned the cows into the corn to graze. That kept the land open all through the winter. Corn exhausts the soil, and open soil blows. The only reason most of those people quit farming here was they had nothing left to farm. The people now know better — most of them, anyway. This is grazing land. And when it's maintained right, it's about the best there is."

Sautter rolled up his window and sat back in his seat. "The only thing we can't control is fire," he said. "Prairie fires are a constant threat, and they're almost always acts of God. Nobody in this country is crazy enough to drop a cigarette on the range. The usual cause of a prairie fire is lightning. Practically all the fires that the Stapleton fire department goes out on are prairie fires. And they can be bad — real bad. I don't know if you've noticed my hands and my neck and chin. That's all grafted skin. I got involved in a prairie fire a few years back — in March of nineteen sixty-seven. It was a windy day, and dry like it usually is, and the grass was about a foot high. I was driving out of town, and I saw some smoke in the hills out south. When a man sees a fire around here, he generally tries to do something about it. We all of us carry a shovel in our cars. Well, I headed that way, and there was a ranch house nearby and I stopped and asked if they had called the fire department, and the woman said she had. But I thought I could do a little something in the meantime. So I went on to the fire. I left my pickup truck on the road and got out my shovel and went through the fence to the range. The fire was burning northwest to southeast. I went down the west side of the fire line, digging and throwing dirt. I worked for about a quarter of a mile. I had it out except for a few stems and chips, and I started back to the pickup. It was then that the wind took a change. It swung around to blowing from the northeast, and it picked up to about sixty miles an hour, and a few smolderings blew into some fresh grass. It went up like a bomb. I was about forty feet from the new line, and it had me cut off from the pickup — it was a couple of hundred yards away. I saw that big wall of fire coming at me, and I knew I was up the creek. You can't get away from a grass fire. You can't outrun it. All you can do is hope for the best and go through it. People have done it and come out the other side. The trouble is a fire like that burns up all the oxygen in the air. It's hard to get a good breath, and I was half worn out from shoveling. Anyway, I ran, but I lost control and I tripped and fell and went down. I lay there — I couldn't move — and the fire burned over, under, and around me. I had on an insulated coat and boots and cap. But my pants, they were permanent-press synthetic — the kind that gets hot and stays hot. And my gloves were in my pocket. So my hands and my legs and part of my face got cooked. I don't know how long I lay there. I got to my feet somehow and got myself back to the pickup — the fire had left me far behind — and got it started and drove till I met the fire trucks coming out from town. The funny thing is it was only then that I started to hurt. They got me into the ambulance and we started for North Platte. Then I really began to hurt. I couldn't wait to get to the hospital, and I thought I'd never leave it. They had me there for three full months, and I hurt every minute of that time until the last two days."

✦

There are one hundred and fifty-five agricultural holdings in Logan County. One hundred and sixteen of them are classified as farms, and thirty-nine are ranches. Most of the farmers run a few cattle, but their principal crop is grain — feed grain and a little wheat. The farms range in size from around a section (six hundred and forty acres) to about two thousand acres, and (for reasons of soil quality and availability of water) they are confined to a narrow belt along the southern edge of the county. The rest of the county is cattle country. There are a few ranches in Logan County of around three thousand acres, but most of them are larger. Small ranches are impractical in the Sand Hills; it takes about twenty acres of such range to support a cow and her calf. Most of the Logan County ranches are profitable enterprises. In 1969, they marketed a total of fifteen thousand five hundred calves, at an average price of a hundred and twenty dollars a head, and received a gross return of just under two million dollars. The biggest ranch in Logan County is owned by Peter Kiewit & Sons (the family concern that also owns the Omaha *World-Herald*) and totals around thirty thousand acres. The Milldale Ranch Company (whose brand — a sort of gothic "H" — is the oldest registered brand in Nebraska) embraces twenty-nine thousand acres, and other important operations include the Logan County Land & Cattle Co. ranch (twenty-three thousand acres), the Baskin Diamond-Bar Ranch (fourteen thousand acres), the Santo Land & Cattle Co. (ten thousand acres), and the Wayne Salisbury ranch, with seven thousand acres of uncommonly good range.

The Baskin ranch is the biggest ranch in the neighborhood of Stapleton still owned by the founding family. Its present proprietor is a tall, leathery man of seventy-two named Robert Baskin. The ranch house is just outside town, a bit north of the railroad tracks and the depot. I walked out and called on Baskin there one Saturday afternoon. He led me across a dining room finished with a Duncan Phyfe table and cabinets full of Haviland china, and into an office hung with family photographs. He put me in a comfortable chair and sat down at a rolltop desk. "Life has treated me all right," he told me. "My dad founded this ranch and got it going, and I've got me a real good son-in-law to carry it on. I mean Dave Jones. Dave more or less runs the Diamond-Bar now, and it couldn't be in better hands. My dad used to say he was planting trees for me. I planted them for my daughter, and now Dave is planting them for their children. I like to think the Diamond-Bar will last. Our brand is an old brand. It's up there close to the Milldale 'H.' My dad bought it off a couple of bachelor brothers from Denmark who homesteaded here in the very early years. He got the money to start this ranch by cutting meat in North Platte and buying and selling Indian horses in the summer. He started out with twelve hundred acres, and he added to it bit by bit — a section or two at a time. I brought it up to its present size. All the ranches around here are made up of bits and pieces. Nobody's ranch is just right. There are always gaps, so you have to cross your neighbor when you move your cattle. I have some good neighbors and I have some not so good. I can get along with anybody who treats me halfway right. But I sure don't believe in being pushed over and walked the full length of. Western hospitality is practically a thing of the past. One of my neighbors had a branding. I went over to help out, and I brought along a couple of my men. Then, a week or so later, I'm branding, and my neighbor comes over to help. But he only brings *one* hand. That isn't what I call hospitality. Wayne Salisbury is branding today, and Dave and two of our hands are over there helping out. Wayne isn't the neighbor I was talking about. We're branding here next Saturday, and I know Wayne will be here with two of his men to help. Nobody can brand without his neighbors in to help. We sell around nine hundred calves a year, and we'll be branding about six hundred of them next week. Everybody wants to expand his operation. Raising cattle is the world's biggest gambling den, and you can't win unless you've got some size. When I was buying a lot of land, back in the middle thirties, you could get it for two or three dollars an acre. Now it's sky-high. It's sixty, seventy, even eighty dollars an acre. The way prices are today, a man can't make a living ranching unless he's already got his ranch. It's impossible to start from scratch. It would mean a capital outlay of almost a quarter of a million dollars for even a little ranch — for only three thousand acres. A man couldn't live long enough to get his money back on an investment like that. And that's just for land. We're all of us mechanized now. We don't need but six or eight hands to run the Diamond-Bar in summer, and in winter there's just two hands and Dave and me. We used to have one man did nothing but ride the range and check up on fences and if the windmills and water tanks were working all right. Some people ride the range in a truck these days, or on a motorbike. We do it by plane. Dave has a little Cessna Skylark. He can check on forty windmills in thirty minutes. I don't mean to say that we've given up the horse. You can't haul a bull out of a spring hole with a motorcycle. And you can't brand and notch and inoculate and castrate without some horses and riders to rope your calves. We have about a hundred head of horses. They're mostly quarter horses. We break and sell a lot of them to stables and such back East. To towns and cities everywhere. There's nothing new about country people leaving the farm and moving into town. But now it looks like the horse is following them in."

Baskin drove me back to the Motel in an air-conditioned Cadillac. He raised a hand in greeting to everybody on the street, and everybody waved to him. He let me off in front of the Cafe. Several boys were lounging there, and I knew two of them. They were the Perry boys — Robert, a senior at the high school, and his fifteen-year-old brother, Monty Joe. Monty had a bandage around his forehead.

"What happened to you?" I said.

Robert laughed. "He got himself kicked by a calf," he said.

"I sure did," Monty said. "I sure guess I did. It was out at the Salisbury branding this morning. One of the riders dragged up a calf, and me and the guy I was working with grabbed him to hold for the brand and the other stuff they do. But he was laying the wrong way. The Salisbury brand goes on the left side. So we made to flip him over and I was holding his front legs and one of them broke loose and kicked me. Those calves are only a couple of months old, but they're strong, and when they smell that hot iron coming at them it's like they get stronger. We had a calf one time that strained so hard he actually ruptured himself. And I guess those little hoofs are sharp. One of the cowboys drove me in to the Platte, and the doctor had to take nine stitches. But you know what? On the way in, we were going about ninety miles an hour, and the Highway Patrol stopped us. But when they saw what the trouble was, they waved us right on. They let us get up to almost a hundred."

✦

The pastor of St. John's Church is a young Nebraskan named John Schlaf. Stapleton is his first parish. "I spent last week where I could see nothing but dead concrete and the hurrying footsteps of man," Father Schlaf told me. "I was at a conference in Omaha. When I got home last night, I felt the difference. I felt the expanse, the space, some reflection of God in the countryside. Down there, I felt closed in — uptight. Down in Missouri, when I was in seminary, I used to think of working in Los Angeles. They need priests there. But then I got more realistic and saw that I was rurally oriented. I grew up a little east of here, in the little town of Spalding. And Omaha isn't even a city in big-city terms. But, of course, I'm a natural celibate. I like privacy. I don't even have a housekeeper here. If I'd wanted a housekeeper, I'd have got married. Stapleton is an ideal kind of parish for a priest like me — a little break for rest and study. I'll be moving on. But I could stay here for the rest of my life and love every month of it. It's a real parish, everybody participates, it's a community, it's beautiful. Everybody knows if somebody needs help, and they see that he gets it. We have some poor people here. They're poor by national income standards. But they don't know it — their needs are small. And if you called them poor, they'd be indignant. They'd be insulted. Stapleton is still remote. The war and the riots and the drugs and the pollution — they seem so far away. And race. Mexicans can't belong to the Elks down in North Platte. That bugs a lot of us, but that's the only race problem here. They've got some Jewish people in North Platte, but I never heard a word of anti-Semitism. Everybody here is sympathetic to civil rights. Of course, it's well removed. There aren't any Negroes in western Nebraska. But if a few Negro families moved into town, our people would lean over backward to be friendly. But if more than a few moved in — I don't know. They'd probably begin to feel threatened. I'm sure of one thing. These are good, Christian people, peace-loving people, but if a hippie group showed up here looking for wild marijuana and everything else, I'd be worried. There'd be bloodshed. These people would stomp on them."

✦

My last day in Stapleton was a Saturday. That night, after supper, after packing my bags, after a farewell walk around town (up to the depot and down to the school), I dropped into the Wagon Wheel Tavern for a farewell glass of beer. There was only a handful of people there. I saw James Morey playing the pinball machine, Wayne Salisbury with a group at the bar, Grace Young at a table with her father drinking a Coke and eating a bowl of popcorn. Elwin Miller and his wife, a pretty, red-haired girl, were sitting in a booth, and they called to me to join them. We sat and talked and drank Hamm's beer and listened to two cowboys with crewcuts and long sideburns arguing about Clint Eastwood (his age and origins and whether he could actually ride a horse or if he used a double) until about eleven o'clock. The Millers drove off to a dance at Mullen, some sixty miles away, and I walked back to the Motel. Except for the cars nosed in at the Wagon Wheel, the street was empty, and the only light was the wild green mercury glare of the streetlight at the Corner and a glow behind the barred back window of the post office. The only sound was the wind — the hot, dry, everlasting wind — stirring the cottonwood trees.

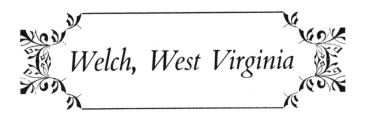

Welch, West Virginia

DRIVING west through southern West Virginia, I stopped for the night at the mountain town of Welch. I stopped there for a night, and I stayed on for almost a week. Welch (population 4,149) is the seat of McDowell County, and McDowell County is Appalachia — the quintessence of Appalachia. It is rich in coal and poor in people. It is the home of a metallurgical coal favorably known throughout the industrial world as Pocahontas No. 3, and the birthplace of the federal food-stamp program. Its mines have never been more productive (or its working miners better paid), but since the mid-nineteen-fifties, when the continuous loader and other automated apparatuses were first introduced, the number of men employed in the McDowell County mines has fallen from twenty thousand to seven thousand. The population of the county has also sharply declined. It dropped from 98,887 in 1950 to 71,359 in 1960, and then to 50,400 in 1970, and many towns that were flourishing at the time of the Second World War are all but ghost towns now. I learned these facts in the course of my stay in Welch. They were not, however, what kept me there. I stayed because of the mountains.

McDowell County is as mountainous as my Long Island home is flat. It covers an area of five hundred and thirty-three square miles, and almost all of it is mountains — big, crowded,

convoluted mountains. There is no ruggeder country anywhere
east of the Rockies. The mountains are steep, with many cliffs
and outcrop ledges, and the slopes are thickly grown with
hickory and hemlock and oak and maple and groves of giant
rhododendron. They rise — eight hundred, a thousand, fifteen
hundred feet — to razorback ridges, and the valleys between are
little more than ravines. Most of the valleys are river valleys,
and most of the rivers are rushing mountain streams. The Tug
Fork River, the biggest of these, has an average fall of ten feet to
the mile. There is very little level land in the county (only two
percent of the total area has a slope of less than twelve feet in a
hundred), and all of it is in the river valleys. So are all the
towns. They are long, narrow towns — a mountainside and a
river, a block of stores and houses, a railroad track, and another
rising mountain. Welch is a maze of narrow streets and old
brick buildings. It lies in a pocket of bottomland at the con-
fluence of Elkhorn Creek, Brown's Creek, and the Tug Fork,
and it is walled around with mountains.

I stayed in Welch at the Carter Hotel. Five stories high, built
of orange brick and white marble, a comfortable relic of the
coal boom of the twenties, the Carter occupies a corner at the
intersection of McDowell Street, which runs north-south, and a
steep, dead-end street called Bank Street. McDowell is one-
way, just wide enough for two cars to move abreast, and
flanked by four-foot sidewalks, but it is the Main Street of
Welch. It follows the course of the Tug Fork River for most of
its way through town. Across the river there is only a railroad
track — a branch line of the Norfolk & Western. My room at
the Carter was a corner room on the second floor, and it looked
south along McDowell. Standing there on my first morning in
town, I could see the U. S. Jewelers, the Flat Iron Drug Store,
Bobo's Barbershop. Then came the mouth of an alley. Then the

flank of a three-level parking garage. Then a five-story red brick building. Then the side of a wooded mountain. That was all. There was no sky. The mountain closed the view.

✦

Every view in Welch is closed by a mountain. "Some of these mountains have names," Hobart Payne, the municipal recorder, told me in his office in City Hall. "They got around to naming some, and some they didn't bother. I guess we've got too many." City Hall fronts on Elkhorn Street, and Elkhorn Street fronts on Elkhorn Creek, and across the creek is the rise of another mountain. "That mountain you're looking at, they call it Mitchell Mountain," Payne said. "Those buildings off to the right up there on the slope are the high school and the junior high. The mountain looks real pretty now, with the trees in leaf and the sun shining down and all. But you ought to see it in the winter. It makes the day pretty short. When I see the sun on those steps leading up to the school, I know it's almost time for lunch. The winter sun don't come over the top of Mitchell Mountain until just about half past ten. And, of course, we don't have it very long. The sun sets here on a winter day about half past two in the afternoon. As a matter of fact, the days aren't any too long here in Welch at any time of year. Sunrise this morning was five-fifteen, according to the almanac, but, if you happened to notice, it wasn't real light until almost seven-thirty."

Welch High School stands far above town but far below the summit of Mitchell Mountain. The steps leading up to it begin at a footbridge on Elkhorn Street which crosses Elkhorn Creek just opposite City Hall. It is a climb of fourteen steps from the end of the bridge to a narrow, hillside cross street of tall, hillside houses. This is Virginia Avenue. Ten more steps and a sidewalk ramp lead to a flight of forty-three steps, and these lead up to

Maple Avenue, another cross street cut into the face of the mountain. A double stairway of sixteen steps circles up and around a terrace to the door of the school, which looks steeply down on Maple Avenue. "We've got four full stories here," William Belcher, the custodian, told me. "Five, counting the basement, where I've got my office. But I operate all over the building, and it's ninety-six steps from here on up to the top. Ninety-six steps, and I'm up there a dozen, fourteen times every day. I'll tell you something else. I grew up running the ridges. I was born out east of town, on Belcher Mountain. But I never knew what climbing was until I took this job. It don't seem to bother the kids. I guess the exercise is good for them. By the same token, this ought to be a healthy town. Everybody gets their exercise here. They can't very well avoid it. You can't walk anywhere in Welch without climbing up or down a hill. And you almost have to walk. I mean, you can't drive your car. Oh, you can drive it, but you can't find a place to park. Most of our streets aren't wide enough for parking. That's residential and business streets both. Some of them aren't even wide enough for sidewalks, and plenty have only one. The few streets here that are wide enough for parking, they're all set up with parking meters. So any place you find to park, it's going to cost you money. The only free parking in town is your own garage, if you've got one. Some people don't. They don't have the space. This town has its faults. These mountains are a problem. But it's like a fellow I had here one time used to say — how many places do you know where you can stand at the basement door and spit on the roof of a three-story house?"

Parking is a municipal monopoly in Welch. Only the town has had the ways and means to produce the necessary space. A plaque on the big parking garage on McDowell Street proclaims it to be "The First Municipally Owned Parking Building in the

United States. Dedicated September, 1941." Two parking
lots — one a little beyond the McDowell Street garage and the
other across town — are also products of municipal ingenuity.
Part of the McDowell Street lot is a shelf across the mouth of
Elkhorn Creek. The other lot consists entirely of a platform
spanning the Elkhorn for a distance of three hundred and
twenty feet (with space for sixty cars), and it is engineered in
such a way that water can flow harmlessly across it in time of
flood. There are, in addition, a second parking garage (on Bank
Street), a third parking lot, and several hundred metered
parking spaces. The rates are low — paternalistically low (ten
cents for an hour in a metered space, and off-street parking is
even cheaper) — but the municipal parking system nevertheless
produces an annual revenue of about a hundred and twenty
thousand dollars. "We don't have a whole lot of crime in
Welch," B. E. Dodson, the chief of police, told me. "Oh, we get
a little breaking and entering, and sometimes a drifter comes
through and maybe tries to steal a car. That's about the extent
of it. I hope it stays that way. I mean, it better. I don't know
how we'd manage otherwise. The Police Department operates
the parking system, and that's practically a full-time job. That's
why I've got my office here in the main garage. I've only got
but twelve men, including my assistant, and we do it all —
twenty-four hours a day. And the traffic. We got no time to
spare for crime. The traffic here — Well, I've been to some real
cities, and I've seen some traffic problems. But you take a Friday
afternoon right here, with the town full of folks looking to
spend their paychecks and their food stamps and their unemployment and their Social Security and their Black Lung and
their everything else — I call that traffic. And speeding. You
wouldn't think it was possible to speed on the kind of streets we
have in Welch, but they do. The kids do. They even some of

them drag. You know Matney's junkyard, out south of town? They won't even take your car anymore. They got enough."

There are six automobile agencies in Welch. They serve the town and most of McDowell County. The largest agency (with two showrooms) is Hall Chevrolet-Oldsmobile, Inc. "We also handle Jeeps," John R. Hall, the president, told me. "This is good country for Jeeps. It's good country for any kind of car. I can sell all the Oldses I can get. These people are crazy about cars. We sell around three hundred and fifty new and seven hundred and fifty used cars a year. We sold a hundred and ten last month alone. And the other dealers — they aren't hurting, either. People really love cars here. Go up a hollow and look at the houses. They're pretty sorry, most of them. But look at the cars out front. Count them. If there's five in the family over sixteen years of age, they've got five cars. A car is something they can spend their money on. It's something to do. They like to drive. They like to drive it hard. They don't care that the roads are narrow and winding and full of holes. You can hit a hole *this* deep on any highway in the county. But they don't care. They don't let that bother them. These people can total a car like nobody else in the world. We've got two tow trucks here and we can't begin to keep up with the wrecks. Look at that red Camaro out there in back. Look at that front end. I don't know if it's even worth repairing. And, shoot, it isn't more than four months old."

Accidents are a commonplace on the hillside streets and switchback roads of Welch and the surrounding county. I read about them every day in the Welch *Daily News* ("Two Injured in Highway Wreck"), and the signs are everywhere — a streak of sudden tire skids, a broken guardrail cable, a totaled car at the bottom of a ravine. One afternoon on Warren Street — a riverside street so narrow that I had to back up half a block to let an approaching car get past me — I counted the splattered corpses of a dog, a cat, two squirrels, and a rabbit. "You can always tell an out-of-stater by the way he handles his car," a state trooper assigned to McDowell County told me. "He creeps. He brakes. He's scared to death of those drops. Some visitors park their car and won't touch it again until it's time to leave. The natives understand the roads. They think they do, anyway. Still, we average maybe thirty accidents a month around the county that are serious enough to call the police. The funny thing is they're very few of them collisions. Most of our accidents, and practically all our fatalities, involve just one vehicle." There was a report of such an accident in the *Daily News* on my second day in Welch. It read:

> Tony Joe (Tommy) Craig, 40, of Welch, miraculously escaped death or serious injury early this morning when a car he was driving plunged several hundred feet off Hobart Street and down a hillside, lodging between a stone wall and the Joe Rucci home on lower McDowell Street, Welch Police Lt. Adolph Bary reported.
>
> The vehicle was demolished, and local police and members of the fire department worked for almost an hour before freeing Craig from the twisted wreckage. He was rushed to Stevens Clinic, where he was under observation for a neck injury. He is also reported to have suffered some cuts and bruises.
>
> Bary said he and Patrolman Estil Halsey are continuing an investigation in an effort to learn the cause of the accident. The 1954 Chevrolet bounced off a high rock cliff and then rolled down the hillside. The incident occurred about 3:30 A.M., while Craig was enroute home from downtown Welch, Bary said.

I read the report as it came from the press at the offices of the *Daily News*. "I'd call that a little unusual," C. H. Hardison, the managing editor, told me. "They don't usually survive. But we get a lot of those over-the-cliff accidents. We've got a lot of cliffs. I had an accident like that happen at my house a few years ago. It was early in the morning, in the winter, in February. I live out south, on Summers Street, down by the river, and a woman came along on the street above and hit some ice on a curve and went through the wire fence they have there and came down my backyard hill and knocked down an apple tree I'd finally got to grow there and slammed into the back of my house. She hit the house at the second floor and then came sliding down, and she took the bathroom window and a whole wall of aluminum siding with her. I called the fire department and the police, and they came, and all they said was 'Get a blanket.'"

I walked up to Hobart Street for a look at the scene of Tony Joe Craig's miraculous escape. To get there, I climbed a street (Court Street) so steep that the sidewalk began and ended as a flight of steps. There are houses — most of them four-story houses — standing shoulder to shoulder on the upper side of Hobart Street on terraced lots secured by a twelve-foot stone retaining wall, and the front doors are reached by flights of twenty and thirty, and even forty, steps. A few of the houses (six in a block of twenty) have garages — little caves dug into the mountain and framed by the retaining wall. Hobart Street is eighteen feet wide, and there is a three-foot sidewalk along the upper side. The other side of the street is a drop of at least three hundred feet to a thrust of rooftops below. I expected to locate the scene by finding a gap in a fence or guardrail. But there is no fence or guardrail the length of Hobart Street. There is only a curbing about four inches high. I never found where the car went over. It could have jumped the curbing at almost any point from one end of the street to the other.

♦

The mayor of Welch is a tall, thin Republican (in a Democratic town) named William B. Swope, and he is also its leading real-estate broker. His real-estate business occupies the ground floor of a three-story brick building on McDowell Street. The upper floors are divided into apartments. "You won't find many buildings here in Welch that don't have a couple of floors of apartments up above," he told me. "People have to have someplace to live. I've done all right in the real-estate business, but real estate is a problem here. We've got a lot of mountains, but we don't have any land, and what we have is rarely on the market. The first thing you want to understand is that most of the land in McDowell County — well, a good third of it, anyway — is owned by just one company. I mean the Pocahontas Land Corporation, and the Pocahontas Land Corporation is a subsidiary of the Norfolk & Western Railway Co. They don't do any mining. They lease the rights to the coal companies and to people like U.S. Steel. They're ready to lease, but they hate to sell. The other big owners — Berwind Land Corporation and Consolidation Coal Company — they think pretty much the same. They will almost never sell you any land in fee. The most you can buy is just the surface. They retain the mineral rights. They're not going to let you have what might be a rich seam of coal. That's only sensible. And the reason they don't like to sell even the surface is this. This country is riddled with coal mines. There are miles of mines right under the city of Welch. And they're always opening new ones. Well, suppose you built a house and the land underneath gave way and the house fell into a mine. They don't want to worry about lawsuits. But the result is a hell of a problem. We don't even own a city dump. We rent five acres in a hollow out west of town. The only sewage-treatment plant in the county is one that U.S.

Steel built out at Gary, five miles south of here. I've got plans for one here in Welch. I've got my eye on a site at the north end of town where we could build an oxidation ditch. Our sewage now goes into the river. I was able to put in a pipe that carries it downstream, out of town. But we'll solve those problems. We've got a good hundred years of coal still left to mine. The big problem is housing. You've seen the houses here in town. There's no such thing as level land, and if you've got a lot as big as seventy-five by a hundred feet you've practically got an estate. I know houses that aren't fit for a hog. Dirty. Fallen down. Hung on the side of a mountain halfway up some hollow. But people will jump at the chance to buy them and fix them up. We've got a hospital here that's offering a guarantee of fifty thousand a year for a doctor. They can't get one. They drive into town with their wives, and she won't even get out of the car. The hills and the roads and no place to build a nice big house — it scares them all away. But God damn it. They don't realize. This place could be another Switzerland."

Mayor Swope himself is comfortably housed. He lives in a nice big stone house with a double gallery across the front, and it stands on a shelf of terraced lawn high up on Mitchell Mountain. I saw it in his company a day or two after our meeting. We approached it along a climbing, winding private road that ended at the door of a garage cut into the mountain slope. The house was directly below the garage, and below the house — far, far below — lay all of Welch. A flight of (thirty-four) stone steps led down to the house. "My grandfather built this house in nineteen and three," Swope told me. "Welch was just beginning then, and there were a lot of highly skilled Italian stonemasons around. 'Tallies,' they called them. The retaining walls you see all over town, the Tallies built them all. Beautiful work. But a lost art now. Now it's all poured concrete, and it ain't worth a damn. It won't last — it doesn't have the weight, it doesn't have the strength. The Tallies built this house. They dug the stone out of the hillside here. They shot and chipped and did it all by hand. It's still as sound as solid rock. I haven't had to do hardly a thing. I *did* put in our road. In my grandfather's time and in my father's time and until not too many years ago, the only way to get to this house was from the street below. That's Maple Avenue way down there, and there are a hundred and sixty-three steps between the street and our front door. My wife and I and our two boys and a girl, we all walked up and down those steps every day of our lives, but we had a winch and a basket on a cable for packages and groceries and stuff. We heated the house with coal. Everything is natural gas here now. That's another thing I've done as mayor, and the city is a little cleaner. Nobody burns coal now except a few miners. They get it at reduced rates by contract. Pocahontas No. 3 is too expensive to burn for heat. Twenty dollars a ton. They only use it for coke. But in the old days you burned coal or nothing, and getting it up the mountain to this house was a problem. My grandfather solved it by having his own mine. A lot of people did the same. Our mine is back there under the garage. It runs back into the mountain for about a thousand feet, and we had a man to dig it for us. He pushed it out on a car on a little track. I walled our mine up ten years ago. We had a miner killed in there. I'll never open it again — not unless I need a bomb shelter."

Most of the best houses in Welch are old houses, and most of them are acquired by inheritance. Few of them ever appear on the open market. "I guess you could say we inherited our house," Rollo L. Taylor, the publisher of the *Daily News*, told me. "We wouldn't be here if we hadn't. We're not natives. My wife is from Alabama, and I was working on the paper in

Spartanburg, down in South Carolina, when we heard that the *Daily News* was coming up for sale. That was in nineteen sixty-three, and we had a baby and we wanted a paper of our own. We came up here and looked the situation over, and everything looked all right — except for a place to live. You've seen some of the houses here. But we were lucky. The publisher of the paper wanted to move away, so we ended up buying his house along with the paper. It's a good brick house, well built and plenty of room (we've got two children now), and we even have a little lawn. A *level* lawn." Other couples new to Welch have had a less hospitable welcome. They have found that the acquisition of a house costs more than merely money. It also calls for patience, vigilance, and an elastic adaptability. "We moved here about ten years ago," Mrs. Edward Jarvis, Jr., told me. "My husband is an inspector-at-large for the State Department of Mines, and we were living up in Fayette County. Then he was transferred to this area. He came down first. He got a room in a motel and started looking around. It took him a month to find an apartment. It wasn't a real apartment. It was just four rooms on the top floor of a house on Court Street. So I came down and we moved in and I began looking for a real place to live — a house. I looked for eight years — eight solid *years* — and then a house turned up out in Junior Poca, out toward Gary. It was the very first house that became available in all those years, and we didn't hesitate. We took it. It's built on a fifteen-degree slope, and there's a long climb up to the front door, but we've got seven rooms, and it's wonderful to finally settle down."

There are about a dozen places to eat in Welch. Most of them are lunchrooms, diners, or drive-ins. I had most of my meals at a clean, well-lighted café (with a horseshoe counter, and tables with tablecloths, and booths around the walls) called the

Mountaineer Restaurant. It occupies the ground floor of a two-story building on a corner of McDowell Street, just down the block from the Carter Hotel, and it is owned and operated by a Welchian of Italian descent named Quinto Bary. One morning, on my way to breakfast there, I happened to look up, and saw that the building was *not* a two-story building. It was a one-story building with a one-story house — a bungalow with a low-pitched roof — on top. The building was red brick, and the house was clapboard, painted red.

I had my breakfast and then looked around and found Bary sitting alone in a booth with a cup of coffee. "Oh, that," he told me. "That was all my wife. She got the brainstorm. We had a house — a regular house — but it wasn't what we wanted. But you can't buy a lot to build on in this town. Even if there was one, it would cost too much. We had this building, though, and my wife got to thinking. It was a good sound building, and the size was big enough — thirty-four by seventy-five feet. I went to a builder and talked about the cost of building something on the roof. The price he gave me, I decided to take a long gamble and build it myself, and I got a real good carpenter that was also willing to try. Weight was one problem, of course. And then there was how to get the material up there on the roof. For that, we built a ramp, like a switchback road, in the back. And to keep down the weight we used aluminum siding. That isn't clapboard, it's all aluminum. We worked out a lot of tricks for convenience. The windows are aluminum, and they lift out for washing. We couldn't stand the weight of a furnace, and the restaurant furnace here wouldn't handle the load, so we heat the house with electricity. We've got three bedrooms, two bathrooms, a big living room, a kitchen, a utility room, and plenty of closets. We've even got a terrace, like a roof garden, in the back. The only thing we haven't got that I'd like to have is a fireplace — too heavy. And the only trouble is that there's too much shade and it's hard to get anything to grow real good up there on the terrace."

✦

There are no farms in McDowell County, and no commercial orchards. A few countrymen keep bees. Driving the mountain roads, I would sometimes see on the slope of a hollow a cluster of white box hives and mistake them for a moment for a row of headstones in a family burying ground. (There *are* a number of family burying grounds in McDowell County, but only two cemeteries. No room. One of the two, a hillside acre near Gary — half Protestant, half Catholic — has long since reached capacity. The only operating cemetery in the county is Iaeger Memorial Cemetery, on a long, climbing point of land at a bend in the Tug Fork River, just below a hamlet called Roderfield.) Even flower or vegetable gardens are rare. They are almost unheard of in town — in Welch. Few householders have space enough in the sun for more than a border of roses or a terraced row of tomatoes. Edward Jarvis, the mine inspector, is one of these. "I've got the room," he told me. "And the slope isn't too bad. I've had pretty good luck with tomatoes and green beans and peppers and lettuce and even watermelon. The only trouble is the mountains. I've got an eastern exposure, and my garden gets the sun for only about three hours — from around eleven o'clock in the morning until two in the afternoon."

One of the biggest holders of tillable land in McDowell County is a wholesale-grocery salesman named Harry Wells. Wells lives a few miles south of Welch, on the road to Gary, and he has around five acres of level bottomland on the east bank of the Tug Fork River. "Let's stop here in the shade," he said to me. "This old cherry tree is a lifesaver on a hot day. And we get some hot days. It's nice and open in this part of the valley, so we're blessed with plenty of sun. Some of these hollows, they're no better than caves. Well, there's my land. It runs on down around that bend, and it's all good loam. No clay. No rocks. No coal. It's been tended for a good long time. I'm sixty-three years old, and my daddy was tending it before I was born. My daddy was a farmer — one of the last in the county. He used to grow corn on that hillside up there across the road. You look like you're wondering how. Well, those days are gone forever. You can't plow land that steep with a tractor. My daddy plowed with a mule. I've never really farmed myself, but I used to tend this bottom. But then I got a better idea. You know how folks live in Welch. They haven't got room enough to hardly even stretch, but a lot of them have that natural urge to plant a garden and see things grow. So I started renting out this land in little patches. I charge them ten dollars for a big enough strip, and I supply the water. I guess I could rent out twice as much land as I've got. Half of Welch does their gardening here. You know Rollo and Annis Taylor? Well, they've been growing stuff here for years. On a summer weekend, this place of mine is full of folks all down on their knees enjoying themselves. Some of them, they'll try anything. Mustard greens. Kale. Broccoli. Okra. Why, there's even some of them growing herbs."

I saw one other garden during my stay in McDowell County. This garden is also out toward Gary, and it is cultivated by a man named H. V. Ashley. Ashley owns and operates a big yellow clapboard railroad boarding house in a Norfolk & Western switchyard on the west bank of the Tug Fork. His place is bounded on the back and sides by acres of sidings and block-long strings of hopper-bottom coal cars, and on the front by the river. A swinging footbridge with a plank floor leads across the river to the road. (There are many such bridges in

McDowell County. "I understand from my undertaker friends that there's nothing like a funeral where you have to carry the coffin across a swinging bridge," Rollo Taylor told me.) I had lunch one day at Ashley's place. The floor was grained and gritty with coal dust, and I ate on a stool at a counter — with a crowd of big, laughing, shouting, starving railroad men — to the rumble of locomotives and the clatter and shriek of hoppers. Lunch was pork chops, red beans, corn bread, and Dr Pepper. After lunch, Ashley took me off in a four-wheel-drive pickup truck to see his garden. It was across the river, across the road, up a steep, sliding, coal-slag cart track, across a cascading brook on a railless bridge of railroad ties, and up a long hollow. We stopped near the head of the hollow at a garden plot about the size of a tennis court. Just beyond the garden were a little square brick building and a huge cylindrical pipe, like a silo on its side. The mouth of the pipe faced down the hollow, and it was fitted with a wire-mesh guard. Through the grille and down across the garden came a driving dynamo hum. "They call this Shaft Hollow," Ashley told me, "and that pipe there is the shaft. It's a ventilator shaft — the outflow from a U.S. Steel Company mine back under that mountain. The shaft is why I've got this garden here. The air blowing out of the mine is a constant sixty degrees, and that makes this end of the hollow like a greenhouse. We're up fairly high here — a couple of thousand feet — but I can put my garden in early. At least a month before the rest of them. And it produces long past frost. You wouldn't believe the crops I get. My sugar corn is six or seven feet high, compared to the average here of maybe four, and the first crop of beans I got last year was over a hundred bushels. I don't own this land, of course. It all belongs to Pocahontas, and they lease it out to U.S. Steel. But they don't care, either one of them, if I use it. They're only interested in coal. Listen how quiet it is up here. You don't hear nothing but that fan. This is what I call peaceful. It's soothing. Well, I'm going to drive you back a different way. It's around the side of the mountain, and you'll get a real nice view — right down on top of my place. My God, I remember one night. I was sitting at home and I heard a noise and I looked out and saw a light shining up on the road. I looked again, and it was a car laying on its back and with one of the headlights shining. I ran out and up to the road and opened the door — and it was my best buddy laying dead across the wheel. He lived up this hollow and he knew the road, but I guess he did something wrong. I'll show you the place where he missed and went over."

✦

On my way back to Welch, I picked up two hitchhiking teenage boys. They hailed me from an unpaved block of houses just north of Ashley's place, and I stopped and they climbed into the front seat beside me. They both wore bluejeans and striped sneakers, and one of them had a basketball under his arm. They weren't going in to town. Heck, no. They only wanted a lift down the road about a mile. They were local boys; their fathers both worked for U.S. Steel.

"My dad don't actually work in the mines," the boy with the basketball said. "He don't like it underground. He says it gives him that whatchamacallit phobia. What he does, he's a car dropper. He unloads the cars that come out of the mine."

"That don't bother my dad," the other boy said. "He likes the weather in there. It's always nice and cool. And the pay is good. It's better, anyway. The mines aren't like they used to be, I guess — the conditions. They're safer, anyway."

"My dad says things are a whole lot better," the first boy said. "And cleaner, too. He says the company used to dump the water from the coal washers in the river, but now they can't.

The state won't let them. He says when he was a boy they used
to dive in the river at a swimming hole they had, and he'd come
up through like a foot of solid coal dust."

"I might go into the mines," the other boy said. "That's the
only thing that would ever keep me here. I don't know. But the
pay is good. And I kind of like these mountains. I sure don't like
it where it's flat. I was up at my cousin's for a while last summer
in Delaware, and it really made me feel funny. It was so flat.
The only trouble here is there isn't nothing to do. There isn't no
place you can go with a girl and park. Where you can be alone.
What you have to do is go all the way out to the movie at
Kimball — to the drive-in."

"That costs money," the first boy said.

"That's what I mean," the other boy said.

"Yeah," the first boy said. He turned back to me. "Well,
thanks a lot. You can let us out at the store up there."

The store was an unpainted shed in a roadside niche in the
mountain wall. The only window was broken, and there was a
padlock hanging open on the door. Above the door was a
homemade sign: "No Lawn Mowers Repaired Here." But the
store wasn't where they were going. I watched them walk
around the car and across to a little spit of land on the other side
of the road. It was just big enough to accommodate a nosed-in
car, and there was a drop all around of twenty feet or more to
the river bottom below. At the end of the spit, a couple of feet
from the edge, stood a ten-foot post with a plywood backboard
at the top and a rusty basketball ring.

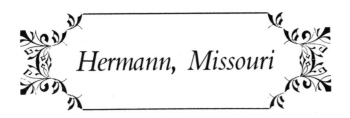

Hermann, Missouri

I GAVE myself the pleasure of an April stay in Hermann, Missouri (population 2,658), an old German town on the rolling south bank of the Missouri River, some eighty miles west of St. Louis. Hermann takes its name from a Germanic hero of the first century and was founded in 1837, on a site chosen for its reputed resemblance to the Fatherland, by the Deutsche Ansiedlungs Gesellschaft zu Philadelphia (German Settlement Society of Philadelphia), an organization created in 1836 by a group of Pennsylvania German-Americans for the purpose of establishing a settlement that would perpetuate German culture and the German language on the free American frontier — a settlement that would be "characteristically German in every particular." By 1839, the settlement had grown from a huddle of log cabins to a town — a flourishing town, laid out on a formal urban plan, with ninety houses, five stores, two hotels, and a post office, and with a population of almost five hundred. Three years later, in 1842, Hermann was designated ("for certain material returns," according to the chief local historian) the seat of Gasconade County. It became a thriving river port ("During those days," a contemporary memoirist has noted, "we were never out of sight of steamboat smoke"), a center of viticulture (for several decades it had the second-largest winery in the United States), and, in 1854, a regular stop on the infant

railroad that grew into the Missouri Pacific. There was talk that
Hermann might come to rival St. Louis as the trans-Mississippi
metropolis. It remained a town. It has never even been more of
a town than it is today. It has, in fact, scarcely changed at all
from the town of its original eminence. Much of Hermann still
looks as it did around the time of the Civil War, and it is still
almost as solidly and determinedly German.

✦

The municipal street-corner trash cans in Hermann are la-
belled "SCHUND," and customers leaving Hillebrand's, the largest
restaurant in town, are confronted by a valediction inscribed on
the vestibule wall: "*Auf Wiedersehen. Kommen Sie Bald Wieder.*"
The former mayor of Hermann (until last year) still carries
business cards reading "C. M. (Cap) Bassman. Herr Burgermeister."

✦

Hermann sits sheltered in a small, semicircular valley, whose
half-encircling slopes were once dense with terraced vineyards.
It consists of twenty or thirty crowded, tree-lined blocks of
well-scrubbed stoops and old brick sidewalks, and a wide main
street called Market Street. Market Street begins at the river, at a
narrow iron-truss bridge (built in 1929 to replace an 1880
ferry), and it extends southward perhaps a mile to the first rise
of the enclosing hills, where it shrinks to a two-lane road.
Market Street has always been the main street of Hermann. It
was named, by the founding Philadelphia Gesellschaft, for its
Philadelphia counterpart, and it was designed by them on a
scale of considerable grandeur. They stipulated that Hermann's
principal street be one hundred and twenty feet wide from curb
to curb — or ten feet wider than the Philadelphia original. I
never got around to pacing it off, but it looks at least that wide.

Parking on Market Street is angle parking, and there is still ample room for four lanes of traffic. Near the southern end of Market Street, there was at one time, around the turn of the century, a big square market building, called the Market Haus, with two rows of produce stalls and a wagon lane between, in the middle of the street; there is now a park two blocks long — with a bandstand, lawns and benches, and an imposing two-story building (until recently the only firehouse and now also the town marshal's office and the municipal jail) — islanded at the northern end of it. The other streets in Hermann are less aggressively proportioned, but they, too, bear the mark of its Philadelphia founders. The distant Gesellschaft required that the streets intersecting Market Street be identified (in the then popular American innovation) by numbers. They elected, however, to give names to the streets running parallel to Market Street. The names they chose suggest some careful thought — Gellert, Franklin, Gutenberg, Schiller, Washington, Mozart, Jefferson, and Goethe. The only street that the original settlers managed to name themselves is Wharf Street.

↓

"That isn't exactly right," J. J. Graf, editor and publisher of the weekly Hermann *Advertiser-Courier* (an offshoot of the *Hermanner Volksblatt*), told me, "although nobody seems to know it. I mean about those street names. Back in the old Prohibition days, the federal agents arrested a fellow here who had a place on First Street. But they had to let him go. The warrant naturally gave his address as First Street. So his lawyer got out the town charter and showed the court there was no such street. The Gesellschaft had named it Front Street."

↓

Hermann is a substantial town for a town of twenty-six hundred people. It has amenities not often found in towns two or three times as large. It has a ten-acre City Park, with tennis courts, playing fields, picnic grounds, a swimming pool, and a handsome octagonal theatre, used for amateur entertainments. It has a modern hospital — the Hermann Area District Hospital — with forty-six beds. It has two medical doctors, two osteopathic doctors (Missouri is the birthplace of osteopathy), two chiropractors, two optometrists, four dentists, and a podiatrist. It has two funeral homes (Toedtmann & Grosse and Herman Blumer) and the Frene Valley Nursing Home. It has five lawyers, a tax accountant, and the Kallmeyer-Schroff Auctioneering Service. It has a well-stocked public library (among the bumper stickers that I saw around town was one that read "Follow Me to the Library") and a movie theatre, the Showboat, with screenings four nights a week. It has the Stone Hill Winery, a recent revival of the relished past, with an average annual production of around forty-five thousand gallons. It has Van Kamp's Boutique & Antiques, the Sound Shoppe, and Klott's Blacksmith Shop. It has a Ford agency, a Chevrolet agency, a Chrysler-Plymouth agency, a Buick agency, a Dodge agency, and a John Deere agency. It has Rohlfing's Greenhouse and the Noelke Jewelry Store. It has the Hermann Cleaners and two laundries — the Helpee-Selfee and the Schillerstrasse. It has a Florsheim Shoe Company factory, a toy factory, and the Hermann Boat Works, home of the Dixie Devil. It has a pool hall (Snake's) and a bowling alley. It has the Sausage Shoppe ("50 Different Types of Cheeses and Sausages") and Schulte's Bakery: *lebkuchen, springerli, stollen, pfeffernüsse, schnitzbrot, streusel.* It has ten beauty parlors, four barbershops, seven bars and the Levee House Cocktail Lounge, and two liquor stores. It also has a resident celebrity — Ken Boyer, the former St. Louis Cardinals star.

✦

"One thing we haven't got," former Mayor (or Burgermeister) Bassman told me, "is an Alcoholics Anonymous. We may be the only town of our size that hasn't. We just don't have that many drunks. Our people are used to Old World gracious living. They grew up drinking beer or wine with their meals. We don't have any kind of extremes. We've got very few people on welfare, and we don't have what I'd call real wealth. I'll admit old Bill Schlender gave us a surprise. Bill was a widower here who died a couple of years ago. He had a shoe store on Schiller Street for as long as I can remember, and he lived upstairs. He wore the same overcoat for forty years, and he used to sit out front of his store in the evening and read the paper by the light of a streetlamp to save electricity. Well, he died and left an estate of seven hundred thousand dollars. Including eighty thousand dollars in a checking account."

✦

Hermann, small as it is, has two distinct (to local eyes) business districts. One of these is the two blocks on Market Street between Third Street and Fifth, with an extension along East Fourth Street between Market and Schiller. The other is East First (or Front) Street between Schiller and Gutenberg. The First Street block is known to Hermannites as Downtown. Market Street and the East Fourth Street block are Uptown. Uptown has Jay's IGA Food Liner, the Sharp Corner Tavern (where at ten o'clock one morning, a day or two after my talk with Bassman, I saw through the open door three gracious livers standing at the bar), the S & S Variety Store, and Schulte's Bakery. Downtown has the Riverfront Bi-Rite Market, the Concert Hall Bar & Barrell, Berlener's Rexall Drugs, and the Sausage Shoppe. The First Missouri Bank of Gasconade County,

the only bank in the area, occupies a classically columned limestone building on East First Street, but it also has a branch office
in a recently restored brick residence (dating from 1871) on
Market Street at Third. "We have a strong feeling about Old
Hermann," Robert C. Kirchhofer, the president of the First
Missouri, told me. "But we don't believe in shrines and monuments. We believe in preservation for use. This is largely why
the bank took over the old Reiff House. That was in 1972, and
I think it's turned out well." He laughed. "I dropped in a few
weeks after our opening to see how things were going, and on
the way out I met an old lady I've known all my life, and she
grabbed me by the hand. 'Oh, Robert,' she said. 'I'm just
thrilled about your new bank. Now I don't have to go all the
way downtown anymore.'"

Some people are inclined to think of Schiller Street between
East Fourth and East First as a kind of midtown. Most of
Hermann's beauty parlors are concentrated there — the Beauty
Bar, Jane's Beauty Salon, Ruthie's Salon of Beauty, Marilyn's
Beauty Salon, and Gloria's Beauty Salon. Gloria is Mrs. Gloria
Bruckerhoff. Her shop is situated in a low, unrestored brick
building (circa 1856) that is also her home. "I guess there *are* a
lot of us girls," she told me, "but we get along together real fine.
There's plenty of customers to go round. The ladies here in
Hermann care about the way they look. They're conservative.
They still like to wear it teased. I try to keep up with things at
the shows in St. Louis, but we're always about two years behind.
Another funny thing is the way all of us girls have started doing
boy haircuts. I mean for boys. I've got boy customers from two
to ninety. The barbers don't like it, but it's their own fool fault.
The boys come to me because I'll style their hair the way they
want it styled. They say the barbers won't listen — they just

keep cutting it in the regular barber way. If you ask me, the boys around here are even more particular than the ladies. I'm even beginning to do those his-and-hers permanents."

✦

The architectural antiquity of much of Hermann is formally and officially acknowledged. In 1972, some twenty square blocks of the town, including all its business streets, were accepted for inclusion in the National Register of Historic Places, Office of Archeology and Historic Preservation, of the National Park Service, Department of the Interior, in Washington. This recognition was largely brought about by the concerted efforts of a number of local groups — the Brush and Palette Club, Historic Hermann, Inc., the Hermann Chamber of Commerce, the First Missouri Bank. "I'm sure it was worth it," Mrs. Anna Hesse, an art teacher and the founder of the Brush and Palette Club, told me. I was sitting with Mrs. Hesse — and with Mrs. William Coe and Mrs. Laura Graf (a cousin of the newspaper publisher), both founding members of Historic Hermann — on the terrace of Mrs. Hesse's home on a slope overlooking the red and green and gray pitched roofs of Hermann. "But, oh, my Lord, the miles and miles of correspondence!" she went on. "I guess you could say that it all began when we organized our first annual Maifest. That was way back in nineteen fifty-two. As you may know, the Maifest is one of the oldest of the German spring festivals. Well, we wanted to try to raise some money to save the Rotunda. That's the octagonal theatre in City Park. Of course, the Maifest goes back to the very beginning of Hermann. But it was originally a children's affair — a close-of-school celebration. I remember — and this was back in the twenties — we'd march from the old German School, on

Schiller Street, out to the park, and there would be the town band and sack races and a maypole. And then we'd have the picnic."

"The *treat*," Mrs. Coe said. "We always called it the treat. But everything was very disciplined. Hermann was totally German in those days, and all of us children spoke German before we learned English. I'm only a Coe by marriage — my maiden name was Dietzel. But about the treat. We would all line up and the bugler would blow a special call and we would march — very correctly — over to the table, and they would give each of us a big slice of knockwurst on a bun. Delicious! Then we'd march away, and in a few minutes the bugle would blow again, and off we'd go to the table once more. This time, they would give us a glass of pink lemonade. And the pink was *wine!* Oh, my! Then one more bugle call, and we'd each get an orange. We really looked forward to the Maifest. But they dropped it twenty years or more ago. It got so the children didn't think it was much of a treat anymore."

"I know," Mrs. Hesse said. "I know. But the Maifest that Hermann is so famous for now is a total community effort. It lasts only two days — a Saturday and Sunday toward the end of May — but it takes months of preparation, and almost every-body in town participates. We usually put on an original his-torical musical at the Rotunda — usually written by Mimi Schmidt. We have a walking tour of Old Hermann, and a tour of several of our most historic homes, and various arts-and-crafts exhibitions, and a parade, and a tasting tour of the Stone Hill Winery, and we set up beer gardens, and there are concerts of old German folk songs, and so on. We've been a great success from the start. Our first Maifest was so successful it was almost a disaster. We did just too good a job promoting it around the state. I don't know what we expected in the way of attendance, but forty thousand people showed up. *Forty thousand!* And something like twenty thousand cars. There was no traffic control. Our police force is only three officers and the marshal. People drove into town from all directions and parked just any old where. Nobody could move. There were cars backed up for miles across the bridge. Market Street was a solid mass of pushing and shoving humanity. I know — I got stranded there. And everybody was starving. Every eating place in town ran out of food by early Saturday afternoon. We didn't know whether to call the Red Cross or the Highway Patrol. I called the Highway Patrol, and at first they wouldn't believe me. They just laughed. I understand that all the way to St. Louis people were taking in strangers and giving them something to eat. It was awful, but we made money — enough to restore the Rotunda, and more. And the next year we were prepared. Everybody in town made sandwiches and set up stands. And practically everybody who came that year brought their own food."

"It's different now," Mrs. Coe said. "We know what to expect. We import enough extra policemen. Everything is organized and controlled. Everybody has a wonderful time. It's been a great thing for Hermann."

"I think it's been our salvation," Mrs. Hesse said. "Hermann would be very different now if we hadn't called attention to our historical treasures. They're what bring so many visitors to the Maifest — our beautiful old homes, our unique living past. And we got started in the very nick of time. The war was just over and prosperity was beginning. The bulldozer was looming. But most of our best architecture was still here, and it could still be saved. What had preserved it for so long, of course, was the Depression. *Our* Depression. We had the longest and the worst of anybody. You might say it began with the First World War. A lot of people don't realize it, but that was the *really* anti-

German war. I remember my parents talking. We Hermannites were practically ostracized. We weren't considered German-Americans — we were Germans. We were the enemy. You may have heard of a village near here called Pershing. Well, its original name was Potsdam. Then, after the war, came Prohibition. And the principal economy of Hermann was wine! Almost everybody here grew grapes for either Stone Hill or Sohns. And we also had two distilleries and a big brewery. Then came the general Depression. I don't know how we survived. Those were terrible years for Hermann. But they did have a kind of silver lining. Hard times kept Hermann a nineteenth-century town. They kept it from going modern, like so many American towns. In a way, they preserved our heritage."

"*Schönheit muss leiden,*" Mrs. Graf said.

Mrs. Hesse laughed. "Yes," she said. " 'To be beautiful one must suffer.' "

✦

"Anna's right about those years," Dr. Joseph F. Schmidt, one of the town's two optometrists, told me. "I came here in the late thirties from Washington, Missouri, which has a big German community itself, but I could see the difference: nothing had changed in Hermann for at least twenty years. I remember a conversation I overheard on the street one day. I'll never forget it. It was two old women talking. It went like this:

"First woman: 'Call me up. I have now the telephone.'

"Second woman: '*Ja? Was ist deine nummer?*'

"First woman: '*Lass mal denken.* Is it two-three-eight? Or is it three-eight-two? You got to get it just right, you know, or it don't work.'"

✦

Hermann has two motels, one at each end of town, and two

hotels: the Central Hotel (a second-floor hotel next door to the Sharp Corner Tavern) and the German Haus. I stayed at the German Haus. It occupies a building (put up in 1847) that was first a store and warehouse and then a private residence. It was remodeled into a hostelry in 1962. It is a rectangular building, two good stories in height, and built of the warm, salmony brick that distinguishes most pre-Civil War architecture in Hermann. Its windows are long and gently arched and hung with dark-green shutters, and it has the steeply pitched standing-seam iron roof of the period, painted barn red. A gallery, reached by an outside staircase, runs along the front and one side of the building. The office of the German Haus, and the living quarters of the owners, Mr. and Mrs. Van Moore, are in an adjacent building, across a graveled parking lot. This building (1841) was the first *Erholungshalle*, or theatre, in Hermann. The office is a comfortable room, always open to guests, with a big round table, a circle of chairs, an electric coffee urn, and three freshly home-baked cakes (usually a pound cake, a crumb cake, and a chocolate layer cake) to choose from every day. On the wall above the coffee urn is an elaborately framed poem, hand-lettered in gold foil on black glass and headed *"Göttlichen Haussegen."* It reads:

> *Wo Glaube da Liebe,*
> *Wo Liebe da Friede,*
> *Wo Friede da Segen,*
> *Wo Segen da Gott —*
> *Wo Gott keine Not.*

Mrs. Moore (née Gellhausen) provided me with a translation:

Where there is belief, there is love,
Where there is love, there is peace,
Where there is peace, there is joy,
Where there is joy, there is God —
Where there is God, there is no want.

The German Haus is conveniently and attractively situated. It stands on a knoll on East Second Street, a block up from the bridge and the river, and it faces down the boulevard sweep of Market Street. I had a big, high-ceilinged corner room that opened on the front gallery, and I liked to sit out there on an old slatted bench in the late afternoon, with much of Hermann spread out around me.

Off to the right, to the south and west, rose the red brick battlements of the two oldest churches — the Gothic spired and dormered St. George Roman Catholic Church and the Protestant St. Paul United Church of Christ, with its seven-story campanile — each on its own imposing hilltop. ("That was no accident," the Reverend Mr. Armin Klemme, pastor of the United Church, told me. "Our two denominations were quite competitive in the early days, and the founding fathers planned with that unfortunate fact in mind. They went to infinite trouble to choose for our churches two sites that had practically the same elevation.") Off to the left, on a bluff above the river, rose the red brick bulk of the Gasconade County Courthouse (the gift, in 1897, of a Hermannite named Charles D. Eitzen), with its colonnaded porch, its four corner domes, and its great central silvery dome ablaze in the setting sun. I could even see, if I stood and craned my neck, the little green bronze cannon (a six-pounder cast in Boston) on its limestone mounting on the courthouse lawn. ("Cannons had names in those old days,"

Arthur A. Schweighauser, a retired vice-president of the Laclede
Steel Company, in St. Louis, and president of Historic Hermann, told me. "Ours is named Ever True. Ever True fired
three shots in the Civil War. This is ultra-Republican country,
as I suppose you know, and it has been since the beginning.
Gasconade County and St. Louis County were the only two
counties in Missouri that voted for Lincoln in 1860. So we were
on the Union side, and Ever True has the distinction of having
stopped the advance of General Sterling Price's Confederate
Army for almost half an hour. That was in October of eighteen
sixty-four. There was nobody living in Hermann then but
women and children and a few old men — the rest of the men
were off fighting for the Union. Price's cavalry commander,
General Marmaduke, knew that. So he came riding up the river
toward what turned out to be the terrible Battle of Westport,
near Kansas City, feeling nice and relaxed. Then, all of a sudden,
there was a cannon shot from somewhere up in town. Marmaduke thought he was being bushwhacked. He stopped and
waited and a few minutes later there was another shot, this time
from a different point in town. Then came another shot, from
still another point. But after that, no more. Marmaduke sent
out a party of scouts. They brought back the answer: a few old
men had been carrying Ever True from hill to hill and pre-
tending to be an army. Well, Marmaduke had his men throw
Ever True into the river. But after he left we fished it out. We
don't claim a victory, of course. I think Price would probably
have been defeated at Westport even without our help.") I
could also see, around one end of the gallery, the superstructure
of the bridge and a stretch of muddy river and, once in a while,
a little white towboat creeping along with its acreage of barges
thrusting out ahead.

But the other view is the view I usually see when I remember my stay in Hermann. That was the view, framed in sweet gums and maples, down the peaceful length of Market Street, across the little bridge that spans a wandering stream called Frene Creek, and beyond — to the cupolaed Stone Hill Winery (built in 1869), massive on its distant hill, and the long green slope and sheltering cedars of the Protestant Cemetery lifting to the opposite far horizon. And I always remember it with the scent of lilacs in the early-evening air and the sound across the rooftops of the bell in the tower of the old German School (now the City Hall) ringing the hours.

✦

I had been in Hermann almost a week before I crossed the Frene Creek bridge and climbed the slope of the Protestant Cemetery. I went, that first time, at the suggestion of Arthur Schweighauser. "I'm sure you've come across the name of George F. Bayer," he told me. "You might call him the founder of Hermann. Bayer was general agent for the Gesellschaft. The Gesellschaft selected the site of Hermann, and Bayer bought the land it was built on. But unless you've read pretty deep, you wouldn't know the rest of the story. The first settlers here had a very hard time for a year or two. They didn't like the land or anything about it, and they blamed it all on Bayer. They made him the scapegoat; they hated him. And Bayer took it to heart. He came down with the fever and died, in eighteen thirty-nine. You'll find his grave in the far southeastern corner of the cemetery. It's up there all by itself. When they buried him, the people decided that there would never be another grave within fifty feet of his. Go up and see for yourself."

I found Bayer's grave without any trouble. It is in the highest, most commanding corner of the cemetery, but it is conspicuous only in its pariah isolation. It is marked by a limestone slab, darkly weathered and slumped askew, with his name, the dates of his birth and death, and a carving in relief of two clasped hands. It was eerie in its reticence. And, in the circumstances, it was hard to imagine what the handclasp signified. I moved away, and was stopped by Bayer's nearest neighbor — a three-foot column surmounted by a sundial. It commemorated a more familiar tragedy: "In memory of the early pioneers who perished in the explosion of the steamboat 'Big Hatchie' at the wharf at Hermann in 1842, the thirty-five dead that lie buried here in unmarked graves and the many whose bodies were never recovered from the waters of the Missouri River."

I started back down the slope to the street below, where I had left my car. It took me almost an hour to get there; I had forgotten the strange enchantment of an old cemetery. Death was taken seriously in America in the nineteenth century. Its presence was accepted and respected, and, with their stylized conjurations of redemption, the placatory memorials it inspired are works of dignity and art. The Protestant Cemetery in Hermann is more enchanting than most. Hermann in the years before and long after the Civil War was blessed with a succession of gifted stone-carvers. Examples of their work are everywhere on the upper, older slopes of the cemetery — a dove in flight toward a heavenly crown, an angel kneeling in prayer, a woman bowed and weeping, a lamb beneath a weeping-willow tree, a skull and crossed bones, a finger (with the legend "Im Himmel") pointing upward, an urn draped with a fringed and tasseled cloth, a ten-foot column rising to a pinnacle cone wreathed in an elaboration, in full relief, of ferns and primroses and lilies. Most of the most richly sculptured stones are also inscribed with richly fervent sentiments. I made a note of one:

Hier
ruhen die irdischen Überreste
von
WILH. DORNER
Geboren
zu Langenwinkel in Baden
Dec. 25, 1807
Gestorben
April 27, 1859
als treuer Jugendlehrer
verband er mit grossem
Lehrertalent, Freiheitsstreben, Redlichkeit
und Biedersein, Friede seiner Asche
I H S

Just below a path that divides the oldest graves from the rest
of the cemetery, I came across the plot of a family named Heck.
It contained three headstones, two of them placed side by side.
The first of these was inscribed

Vater
KARL HECK
geb. 25 Dec., 1821
gest. 20 April, 1915

The second read

Mutter
HENRIETTE HECK
geb. GUENTHER
geb. 28 Juni 1828
gest. 1 Aug. 1901

At the bottom of each stone was inscribed *"In Leben und Tod vereint."* But what interested me was the third stone. It was inscribed

BERTHA HECK
Born Aug. 29, 1851
Died Jan. 31, 1927
Gone but not Forgotten

It seemed to mark the end of an era. I remembered that the *Hermanner Volksblatt,* yielding to the *Advertiser-Courier,* had discontinued publication in 1928.

✦

St. George Cemetery, the Roman Catholic cemetery of Hermann, is on a high and rolling slope on the other outskirt of town, just off Goethe Street. It is a pleasant retreat, with a long *allée* overhung with spreading cedars, and it, too, is rich in sculptured sentiment, but the grave that caught and held my attention there was a new one. It was marked by a small bronze plaque, bright and shining in a glance of sunlight. The inscription read:

FLOYD H. ELSENRAAT
AIC U.S. Air Force
Vietnam
Dec. 24, 1949
Sept. 24, 1971

✦

Hermann (perhaps because of its European roots) is plentifully provided with places to eat. I counted (and visited) eight of them. All were crowded at lunchtime, and two or three were filled at night. They are the A & W Drive-In, at the far south end of town; Imo's Pizza, across the Frene Creek bridge; the Sausage Shoppe (sandwiches and coffee); Schulte's Bakery (doughnuts and coffee); a bar-and-grill on First Street called Mr. R's; and three Market Street restaurants — Hillebrand's, the Central Hotel Café, and the Rockhouse. The Central Hotel Café keeps farmers' hours. It opens in the morning at six o'clock and closes at six in the evening. Hillebrand's and the Rockhouse keep hours more conveniently urban, and I ate most of my meals at one or the other of them. The food of Hermann includes some contributions from the traditional Missouri kitchen (country-cured ham, batter-fried chicken, catfish, cornbread, grits), but otherwise, except for the standard American fast food available at the A & W and at Imo's Pizza, it is wholly German. (A bumper sticker I often saw around town urged "Eat More Possum," but possum was never on any menu during my stay.) I dined at Hillebrand's on my first night in Hermann, and I ordered the evening special. It was a solid, and a satisfying, introduction to the local cuisine — sauerbraten with potato pancakes, apple sauce, and sauerkraut salad. My last meal in Hermann was a home-cooked dinner at the home of the Schweighausers. Mrs. Schweighauser (née Bezold) did the cooking, and the meal she gave us (in a house built in 1846 by her great-grandmother) was an even more satisfying valediction. The entrée was bratwurst with German potato salad. The vegetable was green beans cooked with bacon. There were side dishes of apple sauce and *Schmierkäse*. The bread was home-baked *Schnitzbrot*. The dessert was *Bundkuchen*. With the main course we drank a bottle of dry red wine from the Stone Hill Winery called Virginia Seedling.

I usually had my breakfast at the Rockhouse. It was just down the street from the German Haus — past a dark house in a deep lawn, with a broken bottle and a couple of beer cans under a forsythia bush (the only litter I ever saw anywhere in Hermann), past the Twin Trails liquor store, past Gosen's Gift Shop and Sporting Goods, past Jim's Barber Shop, past a Sears, Roebuck catalogue store, past Van Kamp's Boutique — with the sidewalk roofed or awninged almost all the way. The Rockhouse occupies the ground floors of two small adjoining buildings, the older of which (1842) is built of stone (a rarity in Hermann); hence its name. It is a comfortable place, with a low, beamed ceiling and a portion of the original two-foot-thick stone walls exposed, and the day's special chalked on a slate near the door (ham hock and beans, pot roast and dumplings, Wiener schnitzel), and it was nice to be able to look at the slate at breakfast and decide whether I wanted to come back that night for dinner. And the prices, too, were right. One night I finished dinner (spareribs) and was still hungry. I ordered a chocolate sundae. The waitress brought it, and added the charge to my bill. It was sixteen cents.

✦

Dr. Schmidt, the optometrist, joined me for coffee at the Rockhouse one morning. "No," he said. "I don't mean that. Of course Hermann is a small town. And I hope it will stay that way. What I mean is, it isn't as small-town as it used to be. It's grown up a little bit. I remember when I first came here from Washington, Missouri, and before Mimi and I were married, I had a birthday, and Mimi baked me a cake. There was a woman down the street who used to let me practice on her piano in the evening, and when I went over that night, I took her a slice of my cake. She told me later what happened. She was working at the shoe factory then, and she packed her slice of cake in her lunchbox the next day. At lunchtime, she and her girl friend got to wondering who had baked the cake for me.

My friend said maybe my mother, over in Washington. But the other woman said no. She said, 'I saw Doc when he got off the Washington bus yesterday, and he didn't have any packages with him.'"

✦

There are three real-estate firms in Hermann. One of them, whose red-white-and-blue sign I often saw around town on vacant lots and empty buildings, is the Rathert Agency Realtors. It is owned and operated by Merlin T. Rathert and his wife, Judith. Rathert is a vigorous man of fifty-two. "Exactly, my friend," he told me. "We have a great heritage here, and it needs to be preserved. But with it we must be progressive. We can't be stymied by what is already here. I don't say tear down what we've got. I say maintain it, but plan for the future. I don't want big buildings. Anything over three or four stories is a no-no to me. What I'm saying, my friend, is we've got something here that a lot of communities would like to have. We must keep it, but we must also look ahead. People say don't change this quaint little town. I say grow, my friend. I say don't sit on your laurels."

A day or two later, I talked to Robert Kirchhofer, the president of the First Missouri Bank. Kirchhofer is thirty-five years old, and the youngest president in the history of the bank. "I don't know the answers," he told me. "I think I can say we want to stay small. We certainly don't want to see Hermann spread and sprawl. Take the shopping-center people. They turn up here from time to time, and they want to talk business. We always discourage them. The bank isn't interested in that kind of thing. But we have a very real problem here — a job problem. There are jobs to be had. There are offerings every week in the *Advertiser-Courier*. But they don't pay much more than unemployment compensation. It's the familiar small-town problem.

How do you keep your young people? I was born and raised here. I love Hermann. I want it to stay Hermann. But I'm one of the lucky ones. I graduated from Hermann High School in 1959, and there were sixty of us in that class. I was one of five who went on to college, but only two of us came back to Hermann to stay. The other guy is a farmer. The three others couldn't find any college-graduate jobs here. There aren't even that many high-school-graduate jobs. And I say that ain't good."

Arlie Scharnhorst, the chairman of the board, joined Kirchhofer and me. It was he whom Kirchhofer succeeded as president of the bank. "I think we can survive," Scharnhorst told me. "I think we can keep the kind of Hermann we want. We've always had industry here — the shoe factory and one or two others. I hope we can solve the job problem without becoming really industrialized. And I hope we can avoid becoming a bedroom suburb for St. Louis. I think we can continue to stand on our own two feet. Our economy is sound. I don't know a farm in the area that's in any kind of trouble. Our people are savers. Always have been. There's a tradition here of thrift. That's one of our German virtues. These are ultra-conservative people. Especially when it comes to money. You may have heard what they say around here: 'Never bet on a sure thing unless you can afford to lose.'"

✦

"One of the Poeschels built this house in eighteen sixty-nine," Mrs. William Harrison told me. The Harrisons came to Hermann from Columbia, Missouri, the seat of the state university, and are one of the few non-German families in town. "He was a brother of the Poeschel who built the Stone Hill Winery, and he had some rather grand ideas. This is the only Greek Revival house in Hermann with columns of that size. We've had to

completely restore it, of course. It was in the most dreadful
shape when we bought it, in nineteen fifty-four. A moonshiner
had it during Prohibition, and the people who lived here after
that were too pitifully poor to keep from letting it run all the
way down. We've tried to restore it to exactly what it was
when Poeschel built it. The only real change we made, we
added the fireplace in what we call the family room. Which
brings up an interesting note. The Scharnhorsts, as you probably
know, have the old Charles Eitzen house, which was built
around eighteen fifty, and I'm sure you've noticed those beautiful white marble fireplaces. And Laura Graf, whose house was
built in eighteen ninety-two, has that exquisite Victorian fireplace in her parlor. But our house belongs to a period somewhere in between. It was built at a time when the fireplace was
considered old-fashioned, and the latest thing was the parlor
stove."

✦

The superintendent of schools in Hermann is a big, bald,
sparkling, blue-eyed man named Ross Boeger. "I'm not a
Hermannite," he told me. "I've only been here since nineteen
seventy-three. But Hermann fits right into my background —
I'm a native Missourian, and my ancestry is totally German. I
admire these people. They're house-proud and they're self-dis-
ciplined and they're responsible. When we first moved here, I
saw my neighbor out sweeping the street in front of his house,
and I was amazed. But I soon found out that he was only doing
what everybody does in Hermann. So now I do the same. Well,
our pupils seem to have inherited that Old World respect for
property. You won't find a mark of any kind on any wall in
any rest room in any of our schools. No graffiti — none. And
we don't have any locks on our lockers. We don't need them.
Our people don't steal. Another thing is, the parents here believe

that the school is authority, and they give the school the right to teach *and* to discipline. And this is on top of some very strict home discipline. We do a real job of teaching here, too. Our grading is rigid. I have two children who were still in school when we came to Hermann. They'd always been better-than-average students, but when they started in here they had to work harder than ever before in their lives. I'll tell you something that bugs me. We're told that the young people now can't read or do math as well as the youngsters did thirty or forty years ago. Well, I don't believe it. The difference is this: in the old days, a whole lot of young people dropped out of school very early. They were the poor students, mostly. But now they stay in school, and they naturally pull the average down. I'm really enthusiastic about this town. Did I tell you we start teaching German here in the third grade? It's not a real course at that level. It's just offered, like passing around a box of candy. The German teacher comes into the class one day a week or so, and she starts by saying something like '*Guten Tag.*' Then she tells the kids what it means, and writes the words on the board. The next week, she starts them on '*ein, zwei, drei.*' The kids can pay attention or not. But German is a real course in high school, with an average enrollment in German 1 of around thirty. Now let's move into the shadows. We have our problems here. We have the rumor of drugs. If I were to ask one of our youngsters could he get his hands on some pot this afternoon, the answer would probably be yes. If you ask me is there any in the school, the answer is no. We had a marijuana dog up here a while ago. He was paraded through the halls and past the lockers. Nothing. But by four o'clock this afternoon there'll be a lot of our young people sitting somewhere and smoking their pot. I think we have a little drinking problem, too. But not in the school — not in this building or on any school grounds. School is for schooling."

✦

The *Advertiser-Courier* had had a story, with pictures, headed "TOP RANKING HHS SENIORS." There were thirteen of them — twelve girls and one boy. In the hall outside Boeger's office, I recognized one of the girls. She was Mary Jo Pohlman, a pretty girl with long blond hair and a wide, confident smile. She ranked tenth in the group of thirteen, just ahead of the one boy. "Oh, I'm a feminist," she told me. "I really believe in liberation. I want a career. I'm going to study nursing. But I want to marry, too. The only thing is, I guess I'm also a little old-fashioned. I mean, I like those opened doors."

"Those what?" I said.

"You know," she said. "I like a guy to open the door for me."

✦

I met the Reverend Mr. Klemme, pastor of the United Church of Christ, by appointment, in his office overlooking the river. He is a tall, gray man, with an air of troubled severity. He sat with his back to the view. "I like small towns," he told me. "I feel they represent the best of America. I particularly like Hermann. I'm only sorry that the morals of the city are beginning to reach us here. We had eight pregnancies among our high-school girls last year. But I attribute that to more than moral laxity. By that I mean the problem is complex. Our economy here is very importantly to blame. There seems to be plenty of work, but the wages in all of the ordinary jobs are low. They are often so low that both husband and wife must go out to work. Moral laxity is a direct result of a lack of parental control. There is nobody at home when the children come home from school. And in the evening the parents are both too tired and don't want to be bothered. Our confirmation classes used to be obligatory. Now the parents consult the children. The *parents* consult the *children!*"

The Scharnhorsts are members of the United Church, and Mrs. Scharnhorst (née Heck) is an active volunteer there. She seemed to share some of the Reverend Mr. Klemme's concerns. "Abortion is unheard-of here," she told me. "It isn't even discussed. So the poor girls just go ahead and have their illegitimate babies. And they're only children themselves — fifteen or sixteen years old. Even fourteen! Half the time, they don't even know who the father is. But the strange thing — the thing that is so hard for my generation to understand — is this: it's no disgrace. They're not ostracized. Nobody even seems to mind. Not even when the baby turns out to be half black. Or half white. Or whatever. What worries me is when the father isn't known. Some of those babies are going to grow up and maybe marry their half brother or half sister. And never even know it."

♦

It is generally agreed, though often deplored, that Hermann is a growing town. For all its isolation, its limited economy, the drift away of its young people, its population increases every year. Most of the newcomers are city people — fugitives, for the most part, from St. Louis. Most of them also seem to have arrived by chance and to have settled down on impulse. "It's really almost eerie," Mrs. Bessie Moore, my landlady at the German Haus, told me one afternoon over coffee and a slice of crumb cake still warm from the oven. "People come through here, and something seems to happen, and they decide to stay. I can't explain it. Van and I were born and raised in St. Louis, and we had a successful printing business. I suppose we were getting a little restless. I suppose it's those big-city blues. Anyway, we were out driving through the country one weekend, and we turned off the Interstate at New Florence and wandered along and came over the bridge, and there we were in Hermann. I don't think I'd ever even heard of Hermann. But halfway down

Market Street I had this feeling. It felt like an electric charge. I said to Van, 'Here it is — I've finally made it home!' I said, 'Nothing but good can happen to us here.'"

✦

"I'd call it an accident," Ken Boyer, the former Cardinals star, told me. "I sure didn't plan it that way. Porter Tumy, who has that big farm across the river, brought me down to Hermann in the fall of nineteen sixty-one for some quail shooting, and I liked it here. I thought it was a real fine place. I still do. It has something. I mean besides the shooting. Because there isn't a whole lot of quail shooting left. Too much cow and plow."

✦

The newest newcomers to Hermann whom I got to know were a couple named Tucker — Frank and Phyllis Tucker. Both are in their forties. Tucker is a teacher by profession. Before coming to Hermann, he taught for fifteen years in a suburban St. Louis high school. He works now as a housepainter and paperhanger. His wife is an artist. "We've been here just over a year," she told me. "We had made up our minds to leave St. Louis, and we had heard about this farm near Gerald, down in Franklin County, and we got on the wrong road and ended up here in Hermann. We'd been here before, for a Maifest, and the only impression we had of Hermann was a lot of people rushing around. But this was a beautiful spring day. We really saw the town. And we decided we'd like to see more, so we checked into the German Haus. Then we went out to look around. We came down Third Street and saw this house with Merlin Rathert's sign out front, and we liked everything about it — the lovely block, the lovely pink brick, and the way it's built close to the street, so there's plenty of room in back for a big garden. Frank said, 'Let's not think about it — let's just do it.' So we bought it. I don't know exactly when it was built, but we have a copy of the original abstract for the land. It was a federal grant to a man named Hensley in eighteen thirty-two, and Mr. Bayer, the Gesellschaft agent, bought it from Hensley in eighteen thirty-seven. That kind of continuity pleases me. We bought the house from the estate of an old man named Henry Bohl. Mr. Bohl died a few years ago from a stomach obstruction. The obstruction turned out to be a mass of wood splinters. Mr. Bohl was one of those men who are always chewing on a toothpick. There's a story that he had thirty thousand dollars in cash hidden somewhere in this house. We keep hoping, but we haven't found it yet."

"We could use it," Tucker said. "But the important thing is just being here in this wonderful, friendly town. Phyllis didn't mention why we wanted to leave St. Louis. The high school where I taught was a joy when I first started there. Then something began to change. The community began to go down. We began to get a whole new kind of student. Nobody seemed to want to learn. I'd look at those sullen, resentful faces. It got so I was spending half of every hour on discipline. We had security guards patrolling the halls. And this was a community that had once been the flower of St. Louis County. I went on teaching the way I'd always taught, and when the first set of grades came out last year, there was an uproar. I had failed fifty-two percent of my classes. The uproar came from the students. The principal just sat in his office, trying to hang on till retirement. My classes were impossible. There was always some kid jumping up and threatening he was going to get me. I never actually had a knife pulled on me, but the knives were there. I'll tell you something. If you've never had a girl stand up in class and cuss you out in language so vile you've hardly even heard a man use it — well, if you haven't had that experience, you can't imagine what it does to your insides. I'd go home at night and I wouldn't know whether to cry or get drunk. I decided I didn't have to stay there anymore. And nobody asked me to stay. None of the administrators cared. They thought I was crazy. Quality education isn't the point anymore. The point is fill a slot and keep order. I'm not worried about making a living. I might try teaching again, here in Hermann. It's a whole different system. But I've always been handy with my hands. And I'm beginning to get a reputation for good, honest workmanship. I feel I've saved my soul."

"There's something *Frank* didn't mention," Mrs. Tucker said. "He's probably the only paperhanger or housepainter in Gasconade County with a master's degree in education."

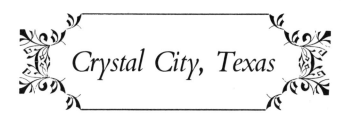

Crystal City, Texas

I CAME down to southwest Texas, down to Crystal City (population 8,104), the seat of Zavala County, where I spent three midsummery November weeks, by way of Rocksprings, the seat of Edwards County, and Uvalde, the Uvalde County seat. Rocksprings is "The Angora Goat Capital of the World," and Uvalde is "The Honey Capital of the World." Crystal City is "The Spinach Capital of the World." It is also, and more importantly, the central city in the fruitful area known as the Winter Garden, which supplies the supermarkets of the Middle West and the Northeast with much of their fresh vegetables — broccoli, beets, cabbage, carrots, cauliflower, kale, lettuce, and onions as well as spinach — between Thanksgiving and Easter.

Zavala County is in a part of the Southwest that to European eyes is as old as New England. Its history, though long, is very largely peripheral. It is possible that the Spanish explorer and chronicler Álvar Núñez Cabeza de Vaca passed through it in 1535 in his transcontinental escape (with three companions) from Indian captivity in South Texas. It is certain that Domingo Terán de los Ríos, coming up from Mexico with the missionary Damian Massanet and an escort of fifty armored soldiers, passed through the area on the historic march, in the spring of 1691, that discovered the pleasant riverine cottonwood motte to

which Father Massanet gave the pious name of San Antonio; the
dusty trail they blazed through the waterless wastes of mesquite
and prickly-pear cactus became, in the early eighteenth century,
the celebrated San Antonio Road, which linked the mission
settlements there with the Rio Grande crossing near the present
town of Eagle Pass. The road served both Texan and Mexican
troops in the Texas War of Independence, and it was traveled
by the many gold-seeking Forty-niners who chose to make for
California by way of northern Mexico; in the early summer of
1865, it saw the romantic passage of General Joseph O. Shelby
and his uniquely unsurrendered Confederate Missouri Cavalry
Division into sanctuary in Mexico. The first permanent settlers
in the area arrived only in the late eighteen sixties, and Zavala
County (whose name commemorates Lorenzo de Zavala, the
first vice-president of the Texas Republic) was organized only
in 1884. It was not until the twentieth century that Zavala
County emerged from the passivity of centuries and its real
history abruptly began. That beginning took place in the hamlet
(sprung shakily up on land made available by the enormous
early-day Cross S Ranch) that now is Crystal City, and it was
occasioned by the discovery there, in 1907, of an abundant and
accessible supply of artesian water.

In a memoir published in the weekly Zavala County *Sentinel*
in 1957, a native son named Ben Jackson remembered that
epochal moment of fifty years before. Jackson at the time of
which he wrote was a boy of eight or ten. "When our artesian
well came in," he recalled, "everybody in town gathered around
it, and there before us was the most beautiful sight in the world.
A great dome of water lifted of its own force and gushed to a
crystal mound above a six-inch casing. Six glorious feet it rose
... paused ... turned ... then rolled outward into a translucent
umbrella and fell as liquid opal into the basin below. From this

improvised pool, it surged to a six-foot ditch. Gallons per minute? I do not know — we gauged its strength emotionally. The water was warm and slightly sulphurous. We all got under it with our clothes on; the drillers held their hands in it as if stroking a silver mane; we drank gallons of it, each sure that no country in the world had water like we had. It felt different. The sulphuric odor was perfume. We lay down in the pool and splashed in it. Babies sat naked and screeching in swirling shallows. Grown women waded in it with their shoes and stockings off, their long dresses pulled up nearly to their knees. Old men sipped it like wine and talked in short sentences as they stood in little clumps and let their quick, green dreams flash through. Beyond the clearing was empire; here was the essence!" Mr. Jackson found it unnecessary to add that it was from that surge of crystalline opalescence that Crystal City immediately took its name.

✦

I came down from the windy hills and canyons of Edwards County, down through the rolling brushland of Uvalde County, down across the long bridge over the muddy green meander of the Neuces River, with its flanking verdancy of giant willows and spreading live oaks and dense pecans, onto the plain of Zavala. The highway ran as straight and flat as a landing strip between hedgerow thickets of mesquite and prickly pear, with every now and then a lavender burst of *cenizo* sage in bloom, and always a pair of vultures drifting high above the road. Beyond the hedges were cultivated fields and cleared pastures and stretches of scrubby range, and beyond the fields and pastures and range was the distant green of farther fields and pastures and range, and beyond the farthest green, at the fading limit of vision, were the sheared horizon and the glare of the milky-blue sky arching up from the vanishing curve of the earth. It was an immensity of land, an immensity of sky — a revelation, an epiphany, of space. (Dale Barker, the owner and editor of the Zavala County *Sentinel*, told me about driving down this highway a year or two earlier with a little girl and her parents from Atlanta. "I watched her sitting there twisting and turning and staring out at everything," Barker said. "And then she turned to her father, and said, 'Daddy, look! The sky comes down *all* around.'") And it was hot. I rolled up the window and turned on the air-conditioning. I never again in Zavala County drove with the car window down or the air-conditioning off.

Crystal City declared itself across the surrounding countryside by a sudden massing of treetop greenery and by the hundred-foot thrust of a spider-legged water tower, shining like a beacon in the sun. The range softened into pasture, into dusty fields. A yellow crew-cab truck stood parked at a break in the hedgerow, and in the distance a troop of stooping men with hoes straggled out along a crop row. The mesquite hedge gave way to mesquite trees. The outskirts of town appeared — the usual outskirts of American towns: a nameless junkyard of cannibalized cars, a boarded-up store, a parade of tourist cabins behind a row of orange trees (Cross S Motel), Kwik Kar Wash, Larry's Bottle Shop, Dairy Queen, Reyes Gro Mkt Beer, Texaco, Gulf, Trevino's Cross Y Café, Bea's Golden Bull Restaurant, and the Casa de Lorenzo Motel. The highway curved off to the right, to the west, and back into pasture and field and range. A potholed city street, with a row of fruiting date palms along one side and a parklike grove of fruiting pecan trees on the other, led quietly into town.

The business center of Crystal City is gathered around a kind of plaza. The center is six blocks long and consists of two streets of shops and stores and offices running north and south and facing each other across a block-wide mall. A branch line of the Missouri Pacific (originally, in 1909, the Crystal City & Uvalde Railway, or, a local historian informed me, "what they liked to call the Creep, Crawl & Uncertain") runs down the middle of the mall between high and flowering hedges of oleander and ligustrum. Beyond the hedges, on either side of the tracks, are streets and parking strips and corridors of lawns furnished with benches and planted with date palms and shading mesquite and Arizona ash and rose gardens and blooming hibiscus and bougainvillea. Here and there among the trees and lawns and gardens, there is always an old man, small and dark and bent, a Mexican-American, hacking at weeds or trimming a hedge or gathering debris into a sack. The street on the east side of the mall is called East Zavala Street, and the street on the west side is called West Zavala Street, and both have covered sidewalks raised a foot or more above the roadway as a protection from the usual blaze of sun and the occasional flooding cloudburst.

I parked my car in an angled slot on East Zavala Street and got out for my first close look at Crystal City. A police car approached, slowed, and stopped. A dark, Mexican-American face in dark glasses looked out — at my rear license plate, then at me.

"New York!" he said. "You are from New York?"

I said I was.

"You have a New York driver's license?"

I said I did.

He held out his hand. "*Por favor?*"

I handed it over. He looked at it, studied it, and gave it back. "*Gracias,*" he said.

"Is there something wrong?" I said.

"Wrong?" He smiled and shook his head. "No, no — there is nothing. I am only interested. I have never before seen a New York license."

East Zavala Street and West Zavala Street, though widely separated, are very largely equal. There are important establishments on both. The Crystal City Municipal Building (with an iconic statue of Popeye, erected during a spinach boom in 1937, on the front steps), the fire station, police headquarters, and the Memorial Library are all on East Zavala Street. So are the Crystal (Rexall) Drug Company, Edwards Furniture Company, an H. E. B. Food Store supermarket, the Shoe Box, Crystal Finance, a Sears, Roebuck catalogue store, Grant D. Mendenhall, C.P.A., McVoy Insurance Agency, Modern Barber Shop, a Ben Franklin store, Service Drug, Western Auto, and the Sacred Heart Catholic Church. The Zavala County Bank, the only bank in town (with the office of S. S. Peters, D.D.S., the only dentist in town, upstairs), and the Winter Garden Cleaners, the only dry-cleaning shop in town, are on West Zavala Street. So are Durbon's Appliance & Furniture, the law offices of Alberto M. Ramon and Rey Perez ("*Despacho de Abogados*"), Audrey's Dress Shop, Speer Jewellers, Harper Ford Motors, the Central Power & Light Company, a J. C. Penney store, Winter Garden Auto Parts, R. S. Gonzales Western Wear, Commercial Refrigeration & Air Conditioning, the Guild Theatre, and Arrañaga's Shoppers World, a supermarket. And so are Tony's Lounge ("Always a Nice Bunch of People Here") and the Zavala Loan Company ("*Prestamos Dinero*"). There are a few businesses, mostly offices, just off the mall. South Texas Construction & Supply ("All Types of Building Materials") is just west of West Zavala Street, the Winter Garden Clinic (a group practice, with two Anglo-American and two Mexican-American physicians) and Paco's Restaurant are off East Zavala Street, and east of them are the Zavala County Courthouse, the post office, the Winter Garden Title Company, and the office of the Texas Employment Commission. "Only, we call it the *Un*employment office," Joe Prestage, the owner of Service Drug, told me. "Because that's what it's all about. And I know it don't look like much, but appearances can be deceiving. It's the busiest place in town."

✦

Crystal City sits low beneath its canopy of trees. Its dimensions are comfortably small, comfortably human in scale. It is as if there were bigness enough in the sky and plain around it. There are fewer than a dozen two-story buildings in the town. These few include the Zavala County Bank, a derelict red brick school (with a toboggan-chute fire escape protruding from an upper window), the Zavala Pump & Engine Company, the Del Monte canning plant, and the Casa de Lorenzo Motel. I stayed at the Casa de Lorenzo. I had a comfortable room (with two double beds and an accretion of paperback books) on the second floor, with a balcony and a view through palms of the boundless western sky, where every evening a sunset kindled and flamed to a doomsday conflagration.

I had plenty of company at the Casa de Lorenzo. With thirty-two units, it is considerably the larger of the two Crystal City motels, but the "No Vacancy" sign was almost always alight. Much of Zavala County is rich in game (deer and doves and bobwhite quail were all in season during my stay), and some of it is also rich in rumors of good-grade oil. Most of my fellow-guests were hunters or oil-field drillers and roustabouts. I seldom saw the drillers and roustabouts themselves — only, at night in the parking lot, their workworn pickup trucks, with battered Louisiana or Oklahoma or distant-Texas license plates. ("I'm so glad you're comfortable," Mrs. Mary Isenberg, the manager of the Casa de Lorenzo, told me. "I wish we could do things nicer here. I'd like to have nicer bedspreads, for one thing. But a lot of our people are oil-field workers. They work hard out there in the hot sun, and they come back here all dirty and lay down on the bed. And, of course, they drink a lot.") The hunters, though also early to rise and early to bed, were more visible. They usually came in from the field, in their equally distinctive cars — their Scouts and campers and station wagons, with their water cans and ice chests and caged dogs, and their guns racked over the windshield — for a drink and lunch and a nap. "That noonday heat out there in the brush, it's a bitch," one of them told me. "Especially for the dogs. Dogs love to hunt. They'd rather put up a bird than eat. No dog really wants to be a lapdog. But they wilt in that noonday sun. And, of course, the only creature that's apt to be stirring out there this time of day is the one creature you don't want to meet. This is rattlesnake country, and this time of year, when it's hot by day and cool by night, is the rattlesnake season. I'm told there are dogs that can smell a rattlesnake at forty or fifty feet. And I met a fellow one time who said he could smell them himself. Had a sweet smell, he said — kind of like a cucumber. But my dogs aren't that kind of dog, and that man ain't me. That's why I wear these fiberglass leggings. It's why I carry an antivenin kit. And it's why I keep looking down as much as up. On the other hand, it don't keep me at home when the quail season's on. I'm no lapdog myself."

Most of the guests at the Casa de Lorenzo ate most of their meals at the motel café. I didn't. ("That whistling?" the cashier told me on my first visit. "That's the cook. But I'll tell you this — be thankful he's whistling. That means he's in a good mood.") I usually walked up the street to Bea's Golden Bull, or drove down to East Uvalde Street to Paco's Restaurant, or went on out south to a restaurant called the Tavern. I generally had breakfast at Bea's. Bea's opens at five o'clock. I was never there that early in the morning, but I was often there by seven o'clock, and sometimes as late as nine, and it was always full — mostly of Anglo-American ranchers or farmers in pointed boots and John Deere caps or big, curly-brimmed hats, sitting in groups of four or five, talking softly, always laughing and joking, drinking cup after cup of watery café coffee. (The first morning I had breakfast at Bea's, I noticed two caps and a straw sombrero hanging on an antler hatrack near the door. They were still hanging there three weeks later. What puzzled me was not why none of them were claimed. The puzzle was where they came from. Bea's customers all ate with their hats on.) "We've got a little different setup here in Zavala County," Dale Barker, the *Sentinel*'s owner, told me. "Our farmers and ranchers don't usually live on their farm or ranch. I don't mean they're absentees. But they live the way I understand the farmers do in Europe. They work their farm but they live in town. They prefer it that way — the whole family does. I know how they feel. I grew up on a farm, and I moved into town as quick as I could. What the farmers do is, they all get up early, but they don't eat breakfast at home. They don't want to. They eat it at Bea's or at Paco's or at the luncheonette at the Service Drug or someplace — wherever their friends eat. Some eat early and then go out to the farm. Some go out to the farm and get things started first. Most of them come back in town again at least once for coffee. Breakfast and morning coffee — that's where we get the news, where we find out what's happening."

In time, I came to know many of Bea's breakfast customers by sight, and there were some with whom I usually exchanged a nod or a greeting. Barker was drinking coffee with one of my nodding acquaintances when I came in one morning, and he invited me to join them. He asked us if we had met. "Well," my acquaintance said. "We've howdy'd. But we ain't shook."

✦

Crystal City, like most other towns in southwest Texas, is predominantly a Mexican-American town, and its cuisine is predominantly Mexican — or, rather, the border hybrid called Tex-Mex. Even the drive-in Dairy Queen offers tacos, enchiladas, and burritos along with its standard shakes, burgers, and fries, and the motel café, for all its transient Anglo clientele, includes chili on its breakfast buffet. Ketchup is available only on request at Bea's, but *serrano* sauce (*serrano* hot chili peppers, garlic, salt, raw onion, tomato) is always on the table. It is as much in demand at breakfast as it is at lunch or dinner. The menu at Bea's (and at Paco's and most other places) offers both Mexican and American (or Texan) breakfasts. I usually ate American (eggs, bacon or ham, hashed brown potatoes, and hot biscuits with the thick, richly floral local honey), and so did most other travelers and visitors. The farmers and ranchers I saw at Bea's — and the businessmen and city and county officials at Paco's — all breakfasted on tacos (in a dozen combinations of eggs and bacon and ham and *chorizo* sausage and potatoes and refried beans) liberally drenched in scorching sauce.

"Chilis are the heart of Mexican cooking," Paco told me one day at lunch. Paco is Frank Z. Galvan ("Paco" is a Mexican diminutive for Frank), and he and his wife, Dorothy, own and operate Paco's. "The reason is that chilis are native to Mexico. There are maybe a hundred different kinds of chili — what you call chili peppers. Go to the market, go to any market here, and you'll see all kinds. Some I never heard of. But the best, the hottest, the chilis we use the most, are *jalapeño* and *serrano*. Another hot one is chili *piquín*. It grows wild all over. We don't use it much. It's too little — about the size of a little pea. Too much trouble to pick. The thing about *piquín* is it's always hot. Other peppers are sweeter — I mean less hot — on the first pick. Then they warm up fast. Garlic is important in our kitchen. So are onions and tomatoes. But chilis are in first place. They are necessary to almost everything you eat here and like. They are necessary to *guacamole*. They are part of refried beans. Our meat loaf. So many chicken dishes — even the famous chicken *mole*. There are recipes for *cabrito* that require it. Our most popular steak is our steak *rancheros* — steak with *rancheros* sauce. *Rancheros* sauce is tomato, garlic, onion, oil, cumin, and chili *serrano*. The same thing with eggs — *huevos rancheros* — is popular at breakfast. I like it myself. It's one of my favorites."

"Frank's *favorite* breakfast is *barbacoa*," Mrs. Galvan said.

"*Barbacoa* is special to Sunday," Paco said. "We don't serve it here. We're closed on Sunday — but also it is too much trouble. *Barbacoa* is like a barbecue. The Anglos around here use brisket of beef, and we use a beef head. A whole head. The cooking is a little different, too. We use a pit and a bed of mesquite-wood coals. But we cook the meat *in* the fire. We wrap the head in foil and then in wet tow sacks, and then cover it with a sheet of tin and fill the pit back up with dirt. That way, no steam escapes. We start at six in the evening, and it's ready early the next morning. When it's done, we slice off the head meat and cut up the tongue and take out the brains and serve it all together with *jalapeño* sauce and refried beans and avocado fixed with raw chili *serrano* ground up with salt and garlic. We have friends who make it. Maybe we can arrange for you to try it sometime."

"We never had beef-head *barbacoa* where I grew up," Mrs. Galvan said. "But I think I'm learning to like it."

I never got to try beef-head *barbacoa* during my stay in Crystal City, but I did once get my fill (almost) of barbecued brisket of beef. And of coleslaw and Spanish rice and refried beans and sliced tomatoes and Lone Star beer. This was at a big Sunday-afternoon barbecue on the firehouse lawn in the neighboring hamlet of Batesville. Half the county had been invited, and it looked as if half the county was there — Anglos and Mexicans, rich and poor, swaybacked sedans and air-conditioned pickup trucks, men and women, children running, laughing, screaming. We all were guests of a slim, smiling, deeply tanned woman in tailored slacks and diamond earrings named Mary Nan West. Miss West is a member of a pioneer Zavala County ranching-and-farming family. "No, this isn't our own beef," she told me. "I had it cut for me up in San Antonio. But it's all prime, and M. J. Blackman is the best barbecue cook I know. I ordered a thousand pounds, and I only hope we have enough to go around. This party is very important to me. My people have been here since nineteen and three. This is a prosperous county, a wonderful county, rich in every natural resource, and everybody used to get along together fine. I mean the Anglos and the Mexicans. And now things seem to have changed. I think that's bad. I hate racial prejudice.That's the reason for this party. It's an annual affair. I started it last year. Everybody was invited, but not everybody came. Some people are shy. This year, we've got a whole lot more. I'll soon be fifty-three years old, and I don't believe that never the twain shall meet. And — God willing and the creeks don't rise — I'm going to keep giving this party until they do."

Driving back from Batesville in the early November dusk, I stopped in an emptiness of brushland to watch the moon come up. I rolled down the window and sat there watching — and heard a faraway sound. It was a doglike bark. There was another bark, and then a banshee wail. Then an answering wail. I knew what it was. I had heard the calling of coyotes before, and it is a sound, a night sound, that one never forgets. Sitting there listening, straining, remembering, I recalled a passage in Ben Jackson's anniversary memoir in the Zavala County *Sentinel*. "All night long," he wrote, "the coyotes howled through the wall holes which were to become windows and doors. You never listen to anything else when a coyote pack is howling. You lie still and concentrate . . . like you do when it thunders . . . or when you hear low sobbing in another room."

✦

We stood in the dappled shade of a big mesquite tree — Stan Snitzer and I — and looked out at an endless field of dusty brown faintly striped with green. Snitzer is an agronomist and the head of a soil-testing concern in Crystal City called the Agriculture & Livestock Laboratory. We had driven out from town to have a look at one of his projects. "I'm from Arizona, and I've only been here a couple of years, but there's one thing I know," he said. "This is a terrific agricultural county. As a matter of fact, Zavala County is one of the largest vegetable-producing counties in the state. And you won't believe this — I sure didn't at first — but there are stretches, especially along the Nueces River, where the topsoil ranges from six to thirty feet deep. Thirty *feet!* This field of onions here was brush just two years ago. I came into the picture because the farmer had a little trouble last year. He had this field in onions last year, too. But, my Lord, the difference! They weren't grass green, like now. They were pale yellow, and not this tall even in December. We took some soil samples and some specimen plants and analyzed them back at the lab, and there it was: low phosphorus and low copper. We handled it with a ground rig, using a fertilizer-chemical spray. And now you see the result. The soil just needed a little help on its way from brush to onions. There are chemical problems, and there are also physical problems. Like compaction. When a field has been worked for years with heavy equipment, the soil tends to pack down, to compact, below the reach of an ordinary plow. That retards root growth and blocks moisture. You have to drag a special long-bladed chisel or ripper through it to break it up. They tell a good story about compaction — might even be true. This was over in Southeast Asia when Uncle Sam was interested in passing along the wonders of American technology to the Vietnamese peasants. Those poor primitives were still cultivating their rice paddies with water-buffalo power. Uncle Sam said, 'Don't waste your time like that. Here, use these tractors.' So they did. And the tractor plows bit too deep and broke up the compacted bottom of the paddy that had taken generations to develop, and all the water drained out."

Snitzer threw back his head and laughed. "I guess we blew it in every department over there," he said. He took out his handkerchief and wiped his eyes and blew his nose. He smoothed his black mustache. "But, getting back to Zavala County, the big problem in growing vegetables isn't just raising a good crop. It's also finding a good market. Growing produce is a big gamble — the biggest gamble in the whole crap game of farming. The farmer needs good luck, and he also needs good contacts with the brokers. He's got to know or guess what's going to happen. You can't store fresh produce. He's got to know what's wanted and when. Take onions. Will the market want Spanish or reds or yellows? Will it want sets or bulbs? He's got about two weeks to maneuver in — to decide whether to harvest his onions as sets or let them go on to bulbs. He can make it big. Or he can go bust. Depending. This field here is about four hundred acres, and my guess is that these onions could gross the farmer between two hundred and four hundred thousand dollars. Or he could lose his shirt. In a bad market, costs can go up to a hundred and fifty percent of the gross. If you can come out with your costs around fifty percent of your gross, you're in good shape. As I say, it all depends. We had thirteen carloads of onions standing on the railroad track in Crystal City one day a couple of years ago. The market collapsed before they even got out of town. They finally had to be dumped."

♦

"Yeah," Joe Prestage commented. "Somebody said if you want to lose your money nice and quiet without anybody noticing, take up farming. I do a little farming myself. I had forty acres of cantaloupes last summer, and about the time they came ripe the market was glutted. I couldn't get two cents a pound in the field. And over at Houston cantaloupes were selling in the stores for seventy-five cents apiece. I like cantaloupe. My whole family likes cantaloupe. But we finally had to turn the cattle into the field."

♦

"Let's put it this way," T. Potter Alger said. We were sitting on the sun porch of his house, a mile or two north of town. Through the windows I could see the shiny green cluster of a little citrus grove hung with golden oranges and big pale moons of grapefruit. "I've been in real estate — farm and ranch acreage — since before World War Two. So I think I know what I'm talking about. Farming may be a big gamble. I'm not saying it isn't. But I don't know of a good farm or ranch anywhere in Zavala County that's up for sale. Which makes me doubt that a whole lot of them are going broke. It's a seller's market for land down here. I handled the sale of a nice piece of land last winter — two thousand acres. It went for six-fifty an acre, and we thought that was a mighty good price. The other day, the fella who bought it got an offer from some outfit in the

Philippine Islands. They offered him a thousand dollars an acre. Farmers like to complain. They're always talking poor. You can get a pair of boots at J. C. Penney's for under fifty dollars. Or you can go up to Lucchese in San Antonio and get a pair made for two or three hundred dollars and up. You'll see some J. C. Penney boots drinking coffee down at Bea's. But you'll also see some Lucchese custom-mades."

✦

"I guess it all depends on where you stand," Del Harp, the manager of the Crystal City office of the Texas Employment Commission, told me. "All I see are people out of work. As you probably know by now, this town is at least eighty percent Mexican-American, and we see about sixty percent of that group. We see some Anglos, too. But it's the Mexicans that keep us busy. We have kind of a different situation here. A lot of our people are summer migrants. As soon as school is out in the spring, the whole family piles into the car and heads north. They work the harvests all the way up into Illinois and Wisconsin and the Dakotas — places like that. They like the money. A family of five can earn around five thousand dollars in just a few weeks in the sugar-beet fields. And they like the travel, the change. But the main thing, of course, is that there's no work here for field hands in the summer. Our summer crops are cotton and corn and hay — all mechanized work. Anyway, the migrants work all summer up north, and then come back here just in time for school. And that's when we begin to pack them in at the office. Most of our winter crops are hand-harvested crops, but the harvest for most of them doesn't begin until November. So they come to see us in that in-between time. Some of them, of course, are with us through most of the winter. I mean, some of them like to work and some don't. But I also mean more than that. There's something wrong with the system. A good man can get maybe a hundred dollars a week in the fields. Or he can stay on unemployment and get maybe eighty. A lot of them figure if they go out in the fields they're working for twenty dollars a week. I ask them, 'Why come back here? Why not stay up north, draw your unemployment up there?' They look at me. 'Stay up there? This is my home. This is where I was born. My house is here.' You never saw such house-proud people. They own their own houses, most of them. Even the poorest of them, the ones that live in the poorest parts of town — what we call Mexico Chico and Mexico Grande. And they most of them keep their houses up. They aren't farmers for nothing. They care about plants, about growing things. They've most of them got their orange trees and their grapefruits and their bananas, and maybe even a date palm. And maybe you've noticed how many houses here have chain-link fences. When you see a chain-link fence, you can be pretty sure that a Mexicano lives there. It's a cultural thing. I guess it's the equivalent of the wall in Old Mexico. It makes the place their own — their *hacienda*. We Anglos don't seem to feel the same way. Not here in the Southwest, anyhow. The thing is, I guess, we're used to owning land."

✦

The senior physician at the Winter Garden Clinic (*"Todo Servicio Médico al Contado Ha No Ser Que Arreglos de Crédito Sean en Adelantado"* — "All Medical Services Cash Unless Credit Arranged in Advance") is a big, heavy man of around fifty named Charles Donald Smith. "I've been here since nineteen fifty-nine," he told me, stubbing out a cigarette and lighting another. "I'm from Missouri, and I came here because I liked it here, and I still do. Most of our patients are Mexicans, and I've seen some changes there. Nutrition used to be a big problem in the youngsters, but the school-lunch program has pretty well taken care of that. The problem wasn't what they ate — as it is with Anglo kids. The problem was that they didn't get enough. The Mexicans eat right. My experience is that Mexicans live longer than Anglos. I've got a woman patient who just turned one hundred and four. When I say 'patient,' I don't mean she's sick. All I mean is that when she don't feel right she comes in to see me. There's never been a time when I haven't had a patient over a hundred. Always Mexican. The last two patients I sent over to San Antonio to be fitted with cardiac pacemakers were nonagenarians. They were a ninety-year-old woman and a man of ninety-four. The man had had a massive congestive heart failure. That was two months ago. Now he's back home here working in his garden — you ought to see the beautiful chilis he grows. I suppose it's the diet. My old patients, at least, they grew up on beans and vegetables and not much meat. In seventeen years, our group here has had just one maternal death. She was a Mexican *gravida* eighteen. Her uterus ruptured during labor."

"Eighteen sounds pretty young for that," I said.

"Young?" Dr. Smith said. He stubbed out his cigarette and lit another. "As a matter of fact, she wasn't very old. But '*gravida* eighteen' doesn't mean she was eighteen years old. It means she was pregnant for the eighteenth time. And her uterus just gave out."

✦

"I don't know how these rumors get started," Edwin A. Lohrmann, the manager of the Southwestern (Crystal City) Division of the Del Monte Corporation, told me. "Why would we want to close this plant? This is a good-sized operation. Del Monte has a total of thirty-six canning plants in this country, and we're right up there in the middle category. This is the *Winter Garden*. It produces twelve months of the year. And so do we. We work the harvests — just like the migrants. We can beans from August twenty-ninth to November twenty-second. We can spinach from December twentieth to mid-March. We can carrots from March thirtieth to May first. We can beets from May tenth to June tenth. We can potatoes from July fifteenth to August fifteenth. We even can some citrus-fruit drinks from time to time. And we're the biggest employer in town. We provide the equivalent of four hundred and twenty-five year-round jobs. We go from a summer low of one hundred and twenty-five jobs to a winter high of six hundred and twenty-five. These rumors — I just don't understand them. I don't see the point."

♦

Warren Wagner and I stepped out on the moonlit terrace of the Crystal City Country Club and stood there with our drinks in the balmy evening air. The terrace overlooked a glimmering swimming pool. ("Nobody uses the pool this time of year," Dale Barker had told me earlier in the evening. "But we keep it full — in case somebody falls in. This way, he only gets wet.") There was a shrill of voices from the bar behind us, and the thump and twang of a country-and-Western band from Uvalde in the big room beyond. Wagner is the biggest and most successful farmer in Zavala County, and he also owns and operates the biggest wholesale-produce company. He looked at me across the lip of his glass — a tall, thin, casual man with graying blond hair cut in a bristly crewcut — and shrugged. "No," he said. "I didn't get to college. My daddy was only a little dairy farmer. I put my farm together with my own two hands. I started out in nineteen forty, at the age of seventeen, with three hundred acres that I got for seven dollars an acre. Brushland. I cleared that land myself, and I paid off my debt at twenty-five dollars a month. I know what bent-back labor is. I've chopped weeds in the heat of the day. When I had forty acres cleared, I put in a crop of spinach, and it turned out pretty good. Then Uncle Sam took me. I came back from the war in nineteen forty-six and started all over again. That didn't bother me. The land I was working was my own land. I hire a lot of labor. Spinach, kale, onions — all our produce has to be hand-harvested. Most of my people are good workers. But the fact is, it isn't their land they're working. It isn't their spinach. They just don't care the way I do. The answer is mechanization. We pick our corn and cotton and cut our hay by machine. I'd like to be mechanized one hundred percent. A few years back, I went around saying I'd pay five thousand dollars for a machine that would replace one man. Now I'd pay fifty thousand, and I have. I've got a tractor that can pull a twenty-four-foot plow. It cost me fifty-five thousand dollars. Anything a machine can do, it does better than a man. A machine can work three hundred and sixty-five days a year — holidays and all. It will work all night if you need to — and we do when we're harvesting corn. It never shows up late for work. It doesn't get sick. It doesn't talk back. And it never goes on strike."

✦

The Allen Fruit Ranch — thirty-five densely planted acres of oranges, grapefruit, and tangerines — is situated on a little knoll, the only rise for miles around, two or three miles south of Crystal City. It was established in 1953 by the late J. B. Allen and is now owned and operated by his widow, Mrs. Vera Allen, and their son, Tommy. I found Mrs. Allen, an attractive woman in rolled-up sleeves and work gloves, busy in the packing shed. "Just look at these tangerines," she told me. "I've spent the whole morning sorting them out. They're every color from green to ripe. I've got a new picker out there, and I swear he must be color-blind. I wondered how he was filling his basket so fast. And now I know. Slam, bam, thank you, Ma'am!

He was just grabbing everything in sight. Pickers can be a problem. I prefer the Latins, if they're any good at all. Some of the whites around here are the laziest hounds you'll ever find. You look out and you see them with an orange in each hand, eating. One drop of rain and they come streaming in for their pay. The Latins can be wonderful. If one offers you, say, a six-pack of beer, you'd better take it, no matter how poor he is. Otherwise, he'll be mortally insulted. If they like you, it's wonderful. They'll come around on Christmas Eve with a little present. The tradition is a dozen tamales made the traditional way — out of a hog head and, if they can get it, a little venison. My husband was in the plumbing business, and he started this operation for a retirement plan. It didn't turn out that way. He found out that he couldn't retire and he couldn't quit. It's the same way with Tommy and me. We just keep running to keep up. But — oh, law! I love every minute of it. We're proud of our fruit. We have customers all over the country. We get the best natural-color citrus fruit in the whole United States. The U.S.D.A. says we grow the best tangerines in the world. They say our ratio of juice, acid, and sugar can't be beat. And look at the size of them. I mean the ripe ones. Here's a good one that that hound must have picked by mistake. Try it and see for yourself. We don't even have to worry very much about weather. A little chill is all right. It helps set the color. We get a drop into the teens only about once in a generation. After all, this is the Winter Garden. As my husband used to say, this is where the sun spends the winter."

✦

Ray Caraveo, the Zavala county agent, and I were driving along on a dusty back road when a big speckled, pompadoured bird, almost as big as a pheasant, popped out of the brush and streaked up the road and ducked into a hedge on the other side.

Caraveo let out a yell: *"Paisano!"* He stared at the empty road, at the dusty screen of hedge. He was grinning from ear to ear. "Now I feel great," he told me. "When a roadrunner crosses your path, it means good luck for the rest of the day. The reason is because *paisano* kills rattlesnakes. At least, that's what I always heard down in Rio Hondo, where I grew up. It isn't too far in miles from my daddy's little farm to here, but it was a giant step for me. I love my daddy, but he could never quite put it together. I was the first person in the history of my family to go to college, and I was the first Mexican-American to be appointed county agricultural agent in the state of Texas. That was in 1970 — the day after I graduated from Texas A. and M. My first job was down in Zapata County, and then I came up here. I've been a lucky man, with or without *paisano*. I have a tremendous set of parents, very encouraging, very supportive. It was my daddy who taught me to work. I have a tremendous wife, one hundred percent behind me. And a tremendous cook. Handmade corn tortillas!" He kissed his fingers. "And I have a tremendous job I love. This is a tremendous agricultural county. Good water. Good soil. And double, even triple, cropping. Which doubles, even triples, the acreage. Things are happening here. Cotton is being revolutionized. They're working on a short-season cotton that will save the grower a month of pesticides and irrigation. They're also working on a wash-and-wear cotton that will be better than polyester — and, with the price of petroleum going up, cheaper, too. And our whole range of produce. Spinach, of course, is still our biggest winter crop, and we'll be seeing some of the best when we meet Bart Wagner this morning. Bart and his daddy, Warren, are quality producers. I don't mean they don't make money. That's what quality often means. I mean they do it both ways. They're into

quality *and* quantity." He looked at me and rolled his eyes.
"And big."

✦

Bart Wagner is forty years old, with brown eyes, brown hair,
a deep tan, and a wide, white smile. He was waiting for us in a
muddy new G.M.C. pickup truck at the head of a rut-track
lane between a fence overgrown with mesquite brush and
prickly pear and a field of brilliant green. He had on a green
John Deere cap and scuffed brown boots. (Caraveo's boots were
tan snakeskin, and he had a braided-horsehair band on his big
hat.) We parked at the side of the road and got out in a blast of
windy heat and joined Wagner in the chilly cab of his truck. A
grid of silvery irrigation pipes quartered the green field, and the
soil was wetly black. We started down the rut-track.

"That field?" Wagner told me. "No — that's kale. I understand it's a kind of soul food. I've tried it a couple of times, but
I didn't really care for it. Nobody eats it around here. It's all
shipped out. It's really a hell of a crop, though. We can get three
or four harvests a season. You cut the leaves but leave the crown
and it sprouts again. It's the same with spinach — except that
with spinach two cuttings is about the limit. This field we're
coming to now is spinach."

Caraveo said, "I don't like all that prickly pear over there,
Bart."

"I know," Wagner said. "It's on the agenda." He said to me,
"The old-timers didn't mind prickly pear as much as we do.
They used to call it south-Texas alfalfa. There was many an old
cowboy saved by that cactus. They'd take a blowtorch and burn
off the spines and feed the succulent to cattle in time of drought.
Your cow won't put on weight that way, but she'll stay alive.
Some old cows get to like prickly pear so much they'll eat it

spines and all. I've seen them out there eating away, with their lips and tongue all swollen up and bleeding."

"Your spinach looks good," Caraveo said. "I think I'll cut myself a little salad. Okay?"

"Help yourself," Wagner said. "We're going to start cutting here tomorrow." He said to me, "Let's get out and take a closer look. I want to show you something."

We followed him up a row of crinkly green. Most of the plants were a good seven inches high. They looked at a glance, like a photograph in a Burpee catalogue, and I said so.

"Maybe so," Wagner said. "But I'm a farmer, and all I see are the flaws. I mean, those little holes — that's beetle damage. Where those leaves are kind of frayed — that's wind-rubbing damage. And here where they're more like torn — that's how hail splits a leaf. No real harm, but you always keep hoping for perfect. Besides, the second cutting is always better. We'll do all right. All we need is a break in the weather."

Caraveo laughed. "He means a bad break for somebody else. That's the best way to make a good living in produce. You get your crop and everybody over in Arizona or out in California loses his."

"The market is just a damn yo-yo," Wagner said. "And it makes you sick to go up to San Antonio and see what spinach is selling for in the store. I don't even want to think about Chicago and New York. But I like it fine at this end. I like a job that keeps me outdoors, I like the independence, and I like being in a basic business. Growing food is real. There's a self-satisfaction. There are a lot of businesses I'd be ashamed to be in."

"Amen," Caraveo said.

✦

"We've got two kinds of customers," George Henrion, the manager of the Crystal City branch of the Southeastern Public

Service (Ice) Company, told me. "And we make two different kinds of ice. One is what we call white ice. The three-hundred-pound slab that that fella's loading over yonder is a bar of white ice. That's the kind of ice the produce shippers use, and that's our main business in the winter. Our season for white ice is the Winter Garden season. It starts in October, when they start shipping cucumbers, and it begins to taper off around the end of April. But during that period we sell Warren Wagner and Joe Byrd and a couple of shippers down in Carrizo Springs an average of four thousand tons a month. The other kind of ice we make is clear ice. That's the ice you buy at the store to cool your iced tea or whatever with. For home use, you naturally want it nice and clear. Now, I doubt if you know this. The faster and colder you freeze ice, the cloudier it is. We manufacture white ice at twelve degrees Fahrenheit in as short a period as twenty-four hours. Clear ice takes thirty-six hours at only around eighteen to twenty degrees. Another thing about making ice that people generally don't know is that you don't add cold to the water. You take the heat out of the water. Now . . ."

✦

There were a dozen laughing, shouting, sweating stripped-down Mexicans working along the loading dock at the Wagner shipping sheds. They were working hard and fast and together in an almost choreographic synchrony. Some were unloading bushel baskets of fresh-cut spinach from a field van. ("We've tried plastic, we've tried everything," Warren Wagner told me, "but nothing can match the old-fashioned wooden bushel for getting produce to market in top-grade condition.") Some were slipping off the basket lids and lifting a few top inches of spinach to make an open center. Some were filling the opening with a shoveled fling of crushed ice. Some were slapping the baskets closed again. Some were heaving the iced and finished bushels up to a man on the tailgate of Frank Kirksey's eighteen-wheel refrigerated tractor-trailer truck. "You notice the way he's stacking those baskets?" Kirksey said. He was a big young man in pointed boots, with his belly hanging over his belt. "He's leaving a little aisle down the middle. That's so when it's loaded they can blow in a sealer of ice for extra safekeeping. I don't use my refrigeration on a load of spinach. I do for cabbage and other stuff. But with spinach you need ice, to preserve the moisture. That won't be for a while yet — another couple of hours. My truck will hold close to eleven hundred bushels of spinach. This is my first load of spinach this year, but I've been trucking spinach for a good long time. And my daddy — it's our business together — did the same before me. I'm carrying this load up to New York — up to a packer in the Bronx. This is Thursday. I'll be out of here by maybe four o'clock. I'll be somewhere in Louisiana by two or three in the morning, and I'll lay down on the bunk in my cab for a couple of hours or so. Gas is the problem — I mean diesel, of course. I try to get from one cheap station to the next. I've paid as little as forty-seven cents and I've had to pay as high as sixty-five. That's a hell of a difference when you get only about three damn miles to the gallon. I drive as fast as the law will let me. I mean, I keep my eyes and ears open. I figure to be home in Amelia, Virginia, by Saturday afternoon for a cooked meal and a good bed, if I'm lucky. Then, if she feels like it, I'll carry my wife on with me up to the Bronx on Sunday. Your friends up East will probably find this spinach in the store by Tuesday morning."

✦

"I've farmed and I've ranched, and all the rest," Jack Kingsbery told me. "I've cowboyed with the best of them. Then one day back in nineteen sixty-three my wife said I didn't seem to be doing much of anything between midnight and four in the morning, so I started up this Kingsbery Manufacturing Company. At first, I stayed close to the local economy. I made all-steel horse feeders and cattle chutes, and calf tables for castrating. Then I invented the Kingsbery Steel Gun Safe. I do business now all over the country. Look at these letters — Michigan, California, Pennsylvania, Alabama, Ohio, New York. And I owe it all to some son of a bitch who broke into my house on Maverick Street and stole four thousand dollars' worth of rifles, pistols, and shotguns. That was in nineteen seventy-four. I kept my guns in wooden cabinets with glass doors, and all a burglar had to do was see them through the window and come in and break the glass. Talk about TV sets and stereos and electric typewriters! Guns are made to order for the ordinary thief. Guns bring almost the full retail price on the hot market. Down in Mexico, they bring better than the original price. I make three different models of safe. That's the smallest standing over there. It's roughly five feet tall, twelve inches deep, and not quite three feet wide. It has a top shelf and three half-shelves for any kind of valuables you might want to lock up, and racks for six guns. I've got others that will hold up to thirty guns and thirty pistols. My safes are all steel, three-sixteenths of an inch thick. They're built like a regular safe, and they're made to be bolted securely to the floor. I don't say they're one hundred-percent burglarproof, but it would take a real determined professional to get one open. And those real professionals don't go around looking for a few hundred dollars' worth of guns. I'm thinking about the loonies and the junkies. I make and sell around six hundred gun safes a year. They sell for just under five hundred dollars and up. Police departments are good customers. They use them for storing guns in evidence. I've never had an unsatisfied customer, but the heck of it is my customers won't speak up for me. They don't want anybody to know they've got a safe full of guns and other valuable stuff."

✦

Bumper stickers are popular in Crystal City. Uncommonly so, I thought. Every third or fourth car seemed to me to carry some aphoristic exhortation or assertion. Most of them were only too familiar: "SAFETY IS NEVER HAVING TO SAY YOU'RE SORRY," "THE BEST LIFE INSURANCE: JESUS CHRIST," "I'M PROUD TO BE A FARMER," "REGISTER MATCHES, NOT FIREARMS." But there was also another I saw from time to time: "RAZA UNIDA — UNIDOS VENCEREMOS." I asked Dale Barker about it one evening. "That goes back to our revolution," he told me. "Back to nineteen sixty-nine. We had some real excitement here for a couple of years. You've probably noticed those boarded-up windows down at the paper. I got tired of replacing the glass. What happened here has also happened in a lot of other Southwestern towns with large Mexican-American populations. The Mexicans got organized and took over the local governments. It was a little different here, though. Everywhere else that I know about, they worked within the framework of the Democratic Party. Here they set up their own party. La Raza Unida, they called it — which means 'united race,' or, more accurately, 'united people.' That old bumper sticker just says that the united people will succeed. And they sure enough did. They had a good leader — a highly intelligent young man, a charming young man, named José Angel Gutiérrez. I've known Angel all his life. He was president of his high-school class. He went to college — to Kingsville, and then to San Antonio for a master's degree in political science, and to the University of Texas, at Austin, for a Ph.D. He came home with a commitment to the Movement. He also had some powerful friends — Chicanos like Chavez. And Father Smith — the Reverend

Sherrill Smith, the pastor of the Sacred Heart Church — was another. The first thing La Raza did was take over the school board. Then they won the city council. And in 1974 Angel was elected to a four-year term as county judge. I try to be objective. I don't think La Raza has run the town much worse than the Anglos did. The Razas came in cold, and they had a lot to learn. They did make one serious mistake. They very foolishly — maybe naïvely — refused to allow a rate increase for natural gas from the supplier in this area, Lo-Vaca Gathering Company. They fought it through the courts, and lost. But even though they lost, the city refused to pay, and last September Lo-Vaca cut off service. You may have read about it. It was in the papers all over the country. Now we're trying to convert to propane. At much higher rates than natural gas, of course."

✦

"You bet," Jack Kingsbery told me. "I went through the revolution. Every minute of it. At the top of my voice. And they sprayed my building, too. Only, whoever did it, what they wrote was 'I Love You.'"

✦

Judge Gutiérrez leaned back in his leather chair and clasped his hands behind his head. He smiled at me across his desk — a handsome man in heavy-rimmed glasses, with a heavy black mustache. He was carefully dressed: polished tan boots, checked tan trousers, a tan leather coat and matching vest, an open shirt, with a thick gold chain around his neck. "I'm sorry I couldn't see you sooner," he told me. "I've been in Washington. I was called to a conference. My long-range plan, you know, is to represent my people in Congress. As a Democrat? Or as La Raza? I don't know. Meanwhile, I intend to run for reelection to the county court. As you may know, the county judge is the chief administrative officer in the county. I'm concerned to reconnect gas service in Crystal City — natural gas. I want to improve the quality of life in general for my people. Zavala County is rich in soil, water, and climate. My great concern is a more equitable division of its wealth. I oppose the concentration of land in the hands of a small Anglo elite. Twenty-six people own eighty-seven percent of Zavala County. What I envision is a cooperative farm, with land acquired through a federal grant. It would provide dignified work for a hundred and fifty of my people, and it would be governed by a board of directors — one of them an Anglo — with myself as chairman. The funding would be minimal — around a million dollars. Joe Byrd has indicated a willingness to sell us land. I consider this plan both desirable and necessary. I want to get my people off welfare. I want them to control their own labor and to earn more. I want them to be able to have work here at home. I want to lift their morale." He sat forward in his chair. "Have you seen my little book? 'A Gringo Manual on How to Handle Mexicans'? Let me give you a copy. I think it will amuse you."

✦

"Well, I'm not one of Angel's great admirers," Ray Caraveo told me. "And he's certainly not one of mine. He calls me the white man's puppy. But I would like very much to see something like his farm plan in operation in Zavala County. Except in one respect. I don't want a cooperative. I know too much about the Russian experience. The home gardens there have always outproduced the state collective farms on an acre-to-acre basis. People work best when they're working for them-selves. I'd like to see each member of the project responsible for a specific piece of acreage. That could be a really tremendous thing."

✦

"Of course, I *inherited* the gas problem," Raul T. Flores, the city manager, told me. "I took office only in July, you know. By then, Lo-Vaca had already taken action to terminate our service. But it's a problem I'm trying to solve. Propane is not the most desirable solution, but I don't see any other choice at the moment. Crystal City is in trouble financially. We owe Lo-Vaca a great deal of money. I admit it. But then what city isn't in trouble these days? So let me say this. I firmly believe that we will be financially stable in — well, in a few months."

✦

"When our revolution took place, I was glad, I was happy," Noemi Cumpian told me. Mrs. Cumpian is an interviewer at the Texas Employment Commission and the wife of an independent trucker. She and her husband have three young children. "The revolution was good for my ethnic pride. I was proud to have a Mexican school board, more Mexican teachers. I was proud to have a Mexican city hall. I was proud to have a leader like Judge Gutiérrez. But now — I don't know. Everything is getting so political."

✦

The Reverend Sherrill Smith came back from the telephone. We were drinking coffee in the dim and haphazardly furnished parlor of his rectory. He is a tall, taut, haggard man in his middle fifties, and he gave me a nervous smile. "I'm sorry," he said. "More parish business. I have no social life whatever. The Mexicanos quite naturally consider me an Anglo. And the Anglos consider me to be deep-down a Mexicano. Or worse — a Chicano. They do agree that I'm a priest. And I am. I grew up in Chicago and I went to Northwestern, but I studied for the priesthood at what is now Assumption Seminary in Sán An-

tonio, and I owe my life in the Church to the late great Arch-
bishop Robert E. Lucey. It was he who introduced me to
Catholic Action, to racial justice and social action, to the
Movement. I came to Crystal City at a thrilling time, in nineteen seventy-two. The revolution was in full swing. I'm afraid
my reputation preceded me. Most of the parish thought I was
some kind of political appointee. The Mexicanos, the ordinary
folk, were distressed. They feared I wasn't spiritual. They were
mistaken. I'm a totally spiritual priest. My social involvement
has always been an extension of the spiritual. I've never used the
pulpit for political purposes. Of course I supported La Raza. I
was enthusiastic. I had nothing but admiration for Angel
Gutiérrez. He was a leader. And yet —"

The telephone rang. Father Smith made a face. He jumped up
and trotted out to his office. He spoke rapidly, softly, in Spanish.
He came trotting back. "La Raza," he said, and shrugged. "I
don't know. Is dissension an absolute of politics? There are now
three La Razas. There is the faction I call the Gutierristas. There
is the faction I call the Barrio Club — the thugs and the vi-
sionaries. And there's the faction I call Los Inocentes. I am now
aligned with the Inocentes. We have the school board and the
city council. We're the middle, I suppose. We have a Mexicano
middle class, you know. Upward-striving. Real Americans. I
hate to say it, but Angel is a heavy-handed man. He doesn't
want just power. He wants to be *recognized* as powerful. Not
everybody is willing to knuckle under to him. Only the rag-
gedies, as I call them, need a strong leader. But the revolution — on balance, it has been good. It was, if nothing else,
psychologically good for the Mexicanos. They needed hope. But
as far as the two cultures are concerned nothing has changed.
Real social integration is a dream. The two cultures haven't
blended. In my six years here, I have performed only six biracial

marriages." He broke off. He gave me a shy look. "I confess to writing poetry. Let me recite a little poem I've written along that line. I call it 'Mexicano/Gringo.'" He then recited:

"Crystal City zippered together by railroad tracks
Keeping their distance/eyeing each other,
Tied together/held apart,
Lying side by side but never touching,
Their meeting in the eye's distance
Merely an illusion."

Father Smith was silent for a moment. "I've been happy here as a priest," he said. "I'm happy to have been involved in political affairs. I've always given of myself. I've wanted to be exploited — to be used. Maybe I overestimated how much I could contribute. I realize now that I'm just another gringo — I'm the priest, I'm tolerated. I wish I could be optimistic. What I'm saying is this: the times they are a-changing. In Crystal City. In south Texas. In the whole Southwest. There's a tide coming up from Mexico. There's a push of aliens. What will this region become? Another Mexico? As an Anglo, I'm very much aware of the push. I don't know about our local Mexicanos. I think maybe they're not aware of it yet. But they will be. Because they're Americans now. I see a hopeless surge of the dispossessed. I see the whole Southwest becoming a rural slum. And, in time, I suppose, the whole earth."

He looked at his coffee, and took a little sip. "Actually," he said, "I'm contented here. I'm getting my head around the idea that this is my last parish — that I'll be staying here to the end. The town is neither friendly nor unfriendly to me. Fortunately, I'm a loner socially. I'll survive. I'm secure in my faith. This is beautiful country. The birds. The flowers. The sun. There's a pond over near Batesville. It's a haven for wild ducks in winter. I go out there as often as I can, and stand and look. Sometimes I get an idea for a poem."

✦

"You'll have to forgive this mess," Owen Williams, the president of the Zavala County Bank, told me. "We're knocking out that wall and expanding next door. But no — I'm not interested in politics. I'm interested in Crystal City and Zavala County. And if I didn't think they were going to survive I wouldn't be spending three hundred thousand dollars to remodel this building."

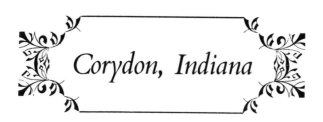

Corydon, Indiana

CORYDON (population 3,107) is the seat of Harrison County, in the rolling limestone hills of Southern Indiana. Southern Indiana is generally considered to consist of the two or three tiers of counties bounded roughly on the east by Louisville, Kentucky; on the west by the Wabash River; and on the south by the convoluted Ohio. The term, however, is no mere geographical designation. It delineates a region that stands geologically and culturally distinct from the rest of the state, and Corydon — situated in a pleasant valley some twenty miles west of Louisville, with a leafy green courthouse square and a population very largely composed of descendants of early-nineteenth-century settlers from Virginia, the Carolinas, and Kentucky — is quintessentially a Southern Indiana town.

Corydon differs in one respect from most other Southern Indiana towns. It has a considerable history. It is one of the three or four oldest towns in Indiana — older, in fact, than the state itself. It was founded in 1808, in what was then the Territory of Indiana, as the seat of the newly created Harrison County. Harrison County was named for General William Henry Harrison, the territorial governor (and later the ninth President of the United States), and it was Harrison, inspired by a popular dirge of the day called "The Pastoral Elegy" ("Sweet Corydon's notes are all o'er / Now lonely he sleeps in the clay"), who gave the town its Virgilian name. Corydon came almost at once to prominence. Early in 1813, the general assembly of the Indiana Territory voted to move the seat of the territorial government from Vincennes, the capital since 1800, to Corydon, and the paraphernalia of government was conveyed to the Harrison County courthouse (which became overnight the territorial statehouse) in May of that year. The rise of Corydon continued. A constitutional convention, called in anticipation of the elevation of Indiana to statehood, was held in Corydon ("in the inviting shade of the spreading boughs of a huge elm tree," as a local historian noted) in June of 1816, and in December, when Indiana was admitted to the Union, the new territorial capital became the first capital of the new state. Corydon served as the capital of Indiana for eight years — until 1825, when, for reasons of geographical convenience, the government was moved to Indianapolis. In the course of those capital years, Corydon grew from a hamlet to a town with (according to a contemporary traveler) "eight or ten neat buildings, besides many others that are ordinary, and a spacious courthouse of stone which is occupied by the legislature during their sessions," and on June 22, 1819, it had the signal honor of a visit by President James Monroe and the war hero (and future seventh President of the United States) General Andrew Jackson. In late October of 1824, the departure for Indianapolis of "an imposing cavalcade of four four-horse wagons" bearing the state records and other property retired Corydon to the unaccustomed obscurity of a country county seat. It lapsed into ordinariness. The veil was lifted only once, and then only for a day. That was on July 9, 1863, when Corydon became the fleeting scene of the one battle of the Civil War to be fought in Indiana. On that neo-historic day, the Confederate raider General John Hunt Morgan and a cavalry force of some twenty-five hundred men, having crossed the Ohio from Kentucky in a fleet of commandeered steamboats, landed on the Harrison County shore, rode swiftly north to Corydon, routed a bewildered company of Indiana Home Guards, paused long enough to extract a ransom of seven hundred dollars from each of the town's three flour mills, and swept on north through an unresisting countryside to eventual fatal collision with a superior federal force near New Lisbon, Ohio, on July 26. Morgan (unlike Sherman the following year in Atlanta) left Corydon much as he found it, and a large part of the town — the Old Capitol on the square, the Governor's pink brick mansion, the State Treasury, the Posey House (Colonel Thomas Lloyd Posey was a son of the last territorial governor), the McGrain House (1808), the Westfall House (1807), the remains of the once spreading Constitutional Elm — still looks pretty much as he left it.

✦

Corydon sits deeply secluded in the bowl of its limestone valley. It is all but invisible from the wooded knobs and hilltop fields that surround it. One can come upon it only suddenly, and then (except by way of a riverine notch on the east) only from the very brink of its encircling heights. I saw the town first from the north, from the top of the mile-long slope that Morgan and his men had climbed in the aftermath of victory so many years ago — a dirt road then, a pot-holed highway now. But even from there the view was guarded. Halfway down the slope was a bridge across a tumbling stream (Big Indian Creek), with a yellow brick house in the early Greek Revival style (the McGrain House) in a broad, wooded lawn on the left and, off to the right, following a bend in the stream, the stacks and rooftops and lumberyards of the Keller (furniture) Manufacturing Company. Beyond the bridge, beyond the grounds of the

McGrain House, the highway became a sidewalked street (North Capitol Avenue) — a tree-hung residential street of comfortable houses built close to the pavement, leading down and down and down to a faraway spread of space, an alteration of light: the courthouse square.

The courthouse square, with its acre or so of lawns and flagstoned walks and benches and towering old sycamores and maples and tulip trees, is the heart and center of Corydon. The old courthouse, the first capitol — a square little gray stone house with an elegant fanlighted doorway and a soaring, steeplelike cupola — is there, and so is the present courthouse, a big, colonnaded brick-and-limestone building (circa 1929). The streets that bound the square — North Capitol Avenue, Beaver Street, North Elm Street, and East Walnut Street — are, and always have been, the principal business streets of the town. The Corydon State Bank, the Town & Country shop, Nolan L. Hottell Insurance, the Corydon (weekly) *Democrat,* the sheriff's office and county jail, the Corydon Dollar Store all face the square on North Capitol Avenue. Across the square, on North Elm Street, are the Masonic Temple, the post office, Conrad & Sons Piano Company, the Corydon United Methodist Church, and the This Is It gift shop. Conrad & Sons Furniture, Griffin's Dry Goods, Berlin's Department Store, the Davis Walgreen drugstore, the Davidson Pool Room, and Albin Jewelers are on Beaver Street, at the foot of the square; and on East Walnut Street, at the head of the square, are the Governor's Mansion (soon to be a museum), the State Treasury (now a private residence), the Presbyterian Church, the Star Cleaners, and Donahue's Café. All the business buildings on the square are two-story buildings, with stores on the street level and offices upstairs, and most of them are brick buildings (many of nineteenth-century origin) painted white or gray or tan or pink or blue or apple green. All of them are fully occupied.

"It's worse than that," Mrs. Hazel Zenor, the secretary and treasurer of the Harrison County Chamber of Commerce, whose office is behind Hottell Insurance, told me. "They're overflowing. *We're* even going to have to move. Nolan Hottell is expanding his business, and he wants to use this space. Well, I've always said you can't stop progress. So we'll just have to grin and bear it. But I never dreamed that this would happen to Corydon. They tried to get Route 135 to go through here ten or fifteen years ago — they said if we didn't get it Corydon would go down the drain. Well, we didn't get it. Then they said if they allowed that shopping center to go up just north of town, that could put our downtown on its back. Well, there isn't an inch of space to rent anywhere around the square, and they've got two vacancies at the shopping center. The answer, of course, is Louisville. We've got Interstate 64 now, and that brings Louisville close. Our people are finding they can live in Corydon and work in Louisville — at General Electric or Ford or one of the other big plants. And a lot of Louisville people are getting tired of city life and that busing they've got up there, and are moving down here to Corydon. So the result is that we've got progress. I only wish we didn't have to find ourselves a new office."

"Hazel is right," Arville L. Funk, a member of the law firm of Hays, O'Bannon & Funk, with offices on the second floor of the Corydon *Democrat* building (circa 1860), told me. "We've got progress happening here. And we do call it progress. I hope it won't change the character of Corydon — I know it won't. Our problem has always been to keep our young people — it's the problem that faces every small town these days. And now

Louisville is providing us with a good solution. I think there are worse things than being a bedroom community. But I really want us to be more than that. I'm a native of Corydon — the first Funk came through here with George Rogers Clark in 1778. I lived and practiced law in Indianapolis for fifteen years. And all that time, when somebody would ask me where I lived, I would always say I was from Corydon. I never thought of Indianapolis as permanent. I was a transient there all those years. I got married there, I owned two different houses there, but all the time I was really just living out of a suitcase. Then I got the opportunity to come home. I love Corydon. I'm a strong environmentalist, and my hobby is local history. I think we're combining the preservation of our good things with staying alive as a town. We've kept our downtown, we don't have any chain stores there, we have a continuity of ownership that makes for commercial stability. You come back here twenty-five years from now and I think you'll find our square will still be here. We've got countywide zoning, we know what kind of industry we want, and we know where we want to put it. We're not going overboard to bring in factories. We've got a factory — we've got the furniture factory. It's our big industry, it employs seven hundred and fifty people, and it's part of our scene — it's been here almost a hundred years. What we want is warehousing, that kind of thing. We look at more than the profit figures. We have a little railroad here — a little seven-mile spur line called the Louisville, New Albany and Corydon — and we've had it for almost a hundred years. It used to run all the way to Louisville. Now it's part of the Southern system. It's only a freight line now, of course. And its only real customer is Keller. Anyway, a few years ago, when they were planning Interstate 64, just north of here, there was the problem of the railroad. It crossed the Interstate, and the state didn't want to build an overpass. So the state said, 'Let's buy their railroad and junk it — be a lot cheaper.' But we didn't want that. And Bill Buchanan, who owned the railroad, didn't want that, either. So we've still got our railroad. We've still got the Corydon we love. And the reason is that we've done a whole bunch of things right."

"What Art Funk says is true," Blaine Wiseman, the president of the Old Capital Bank & Trust Company, told me. "This is the fourth-fastest-growing county in the state of Indiana, but we know that the industrial game in rural communities is changing. It used to be what was wanted was P.R.M. and R. Now it's P.P.T.L. The old way was Pure Raw Materials and Railroads. The new thing is Pretty Place to Live. There's a whole lot of executives' wives these days that won't move to a community unless it has a good environment."

♦

Corydon has three hostelries. One — and the only one near the center of town — is a small, partly residential hotel just west of the square called the Hotel Corydon. The others are the Lincoln Hills Motel, a conventional motel on the western edge of town, and the Old Capitol Inn, a big, new (1973) clapboard-and-stone hotel in a functional imitation of the local Greek Revival style, about two miles north of town. I stayed at the Old Capitol Inn, in a quiet back room on the second floor with a view, across a parking strip, of the Louisville, New Albany & Corydon Railroad tracks and — once every few days — a leisurely little freight train.

"I'm sure you're very comfortable there," Frederick P. Griffin, the owner of Griffin's Dry Goods, told me. "I know they set a good table. We're proud of the inn. It's part of the progress that's happening here in Corydon. And we're proud of Larry and Olivia Orme, the nice young people who own it. Olivia was a Miller, and Orme is an old name around here. And I think you'll be interested in this: Back in the old capital days, the place everybody stayed, the legislators and all, was Conrad's Tavern, later called the Old Capitol Hotel, and it was way out of town, too — out east on the Old Plank Road. Now, why did they build it way out there? Well, sir, it was for the same reason that the inn is where it is. Larry and Olivia had to have plenty of room for their guests to park. So did the old hotel. Everybody traveled on horseback back in eighteen sixteen, and the old hotel had to have enough land to pasture all those horses."

The lobby of the inn, as well as its Heritage Cocktail Lounge ("Our dress code will not permit shorts, halter tops, T-shirts, tank tops, and you must wear shoes"), its Squire Boone Coffee Shop (with a portrait of Squire Boone, a younger brother of Daniel), and its General Harrison Dining Room (Windsor chairs, flock wallpaper, brass chandeliers and sconces), is furnished and decorated in the Corydon period style. "I wish we could have done more," Olivia Orme told me. "We wanted fireplaces in the lobby and in the dining room, but we were getting into too many cost overruns. We *were* able to do a few nice things. I hope you've noticed the decorated china in the dining room, and our heavy period cutlery. I think our silver is really lovely. But, oh dear, we have such a terrible time keeping it on the table. Larry and I used to wonder why so many even good hotels and restaurants had such ordinary table silver. Well, now we know. Any object that has any kind of emblem or insignia or monogram on it is fair game. It's given us a very poor opinion of people. But I won't compromise — not yet."

Corydon is not richly supplied with outstanding places to eat. Lunch is the only meal that most Corydonians ever eat away from home, and most places to eat in Corydon are merely eating places. The General Harrison Dining Room is the only real restaurant. I found only three or four places to eat that were in or near the center of town. One of these, Donahue's Café, is on the square. The others are on Chestnut Street, a block below the square. They are the Elm Restaurant ("Home Cooked Meals & Pies, Open 6 days — 5 A.M. to 8 P.M."), the Ideal Cafeteria (which closes at eight in the evening), and Jock's Lunch. The rest of Corydon's eating places all seem to be on the outskirts of town and are fast-food operations. They include a Kentucky Fried Chicken, a Burger Queen, Duffy's, the Kool Panther, and the Seafood House. The Seafood House ("The Largest Fish Sandwich in Town") was the only one of these that I cared to try more than once. I usually had the specialty of the house: a fried-fish sandwich with a side order of hush puppies and a glass of Big Red cream soda. (On my first visit there, I asked the waitress what kind of fish they used — was it local catfish? She shook her head. "I don't think so," she said. "I think it's just plain fish.") I always breakfasted and generally dined at the Old Capitol Inn. The Ormes, as Griffin said, set a good table — especially at breakfast. The ham and the bacon both were country-cured, the biscuits were light and hot, and the eggs were the sweetest, the freshest, I have ever had.

✦

Jack Washburn picked up a pencil and rolled it slowly back and forth between his fingers. He is the Harrison County extension agent, and we were sitting in his upstairs office on Beaver Street. "Well," he told me, "Harrison County is hard-scrabble farming. I was born in Texas and raised in Arkansas, and that's what I have to call it. There's good land here, of course, but a whole lot of it is hills and trees. So the natural result is a lot of hay production and hog farming — a lot of ham and bacon. And also a lot of chicken-and-egg production. Harrison County used to call itself the chicken capital of the world. We've still got a whole bunch of hatcheries, and, of course, we've got a big poultry-processing plant — Arpac — right here in town. I guess, after Keller's Arpac is our biggest employer. They've got a lot of people raising chickens for them. It's a big operation." He tossed the pencil back on his desk. He sat up straight. His eyes brightened. "But there's something happening here that's new. It's really new and really significant. Our average farm is only a little over a hundred acres, and it's been a good long time since a farm that size was self-supporting. But people still like to farm — to live on a farm and grow things, to get in touch with the basics. There's more of them every year. And they've worked out something here that I call noncommercial farming. It's a whole new life-style. What makes it possible here is Louisville — the jobs of all kinds that are available there. The Louisville job is the farmer's main income, and the farm is his way of life. I've got a family, distant neighbors of mine, in mind. They're a good example. Charlie is married, with two boys, and they have about a hundred acres. It's high land, rolling, some of it woods, none of it real level. Charlie has fifteen acres in corn, and he feeds two hundred hogs. He keeps fifteen or sixteen cows and a bull, and they yield him fifteen or sixteen calves a year. He has four horses — for riding, for pleasure. He has his vegetable garden, and he also raises chickens for meat and eggs. I think he has some fruit trees, and he keeps a hive or two of bees. I said his place was well wooded. That's not all bad. He heats with wood, and he cuts and sells maybe five loads of wood a year for fuel and lumber and maybe some walnut veneer. He fishes when he can — you can find good fishing for bass and bluegill and catfish almost anywhere around here — and he shoots some quail and wild turkey in season, and he usually gets his deer in the fall. He gets up at four o'clock in the morning, does chores and has his breakfast, and goes to work at seven. Charlie works at one of the plants in Louisville. He's home by four o'clock. He does evening chores, eats dinner, and is usually in bed by eight. His wife also works. She has a part-time job here in town. The boys are still in school, but they have their chores, their responsibilities at home. Now, here's the way it works out: Charlie gets maybe nine thousand dollars a year from his Louisville job, and his wife makes around four. His hogs bring in maybe fifteen hundred, his calves maybe a thousand, and his wood another thousand. On top of that, he probably sells some fruit and vegetables from time to time. And, on top of that, he owns his house and farm, and he raises most of his own food. Charlie thinks he's doing pretty good. His kids are growing up right. They're into our 4-H program, they each raise a hog or a calf of their own for spending money. They ride and they hunt and fish with their daddy." Washburn picked up his pencil and began to roll it again. "So that's the way it works. Charlie doesn't call his life an easy life, and I don't either. Nobody likes to stay up all night with a sick cow. But there's work and there's labor. Labor is drudgery. Charlie works, and work is satisfying. It's basic. Charlie doesn't have to keep in shape by jogging or running or joining a tennis club. He lives in shape. But the point of it all is this: Charlie is only one of many. The noncommercial farm is taking over here. I see new farmers every week or two — young people, no farming background whatever, a lot of them city people. They're getting out of the mainstream. They've decided they would rather work than labor. They want to enjoy their life."

✦

Randy West, the managing editor of the Corydon *Democrat*, smiled up at the waitress and called her by name. "Just coffee," he said. We were sitting in a pewlike wooden booth at Jock's Lunch. It was ten o'clock on a muggy, drizzling morning, and the place was crowded. "That's why I brought you here," West told me. He is a small young man with a big brown beard and bland hazel eyes. "Corydon is the epicenter of Harrison County, and Jock's is the epicenter of Corydon — every weekday morning, anyway. Everybody who is anybody comes here for his morning coffee. I know it isn't much to look at, but neither is Woody Allen. That man there at the end of the counter is our county prosecutor. The one sitting next to him is a former junior-high-school principal. He's talking to a professional conservationist. The man with a hat on eating a piece of pie is a big architect from New Albany. The man next to him, that colored man, is Anderson Perry. He's been shining shoes at the poolroom for at least forty years. Back there at that table is the manager of Walgreen's. And that's Jock himself, in the white shirt and apron, holding court with two insurance men and a lawyer. Jock's real name is Paul — Paul Timberlake. When he isn't working here at the café, he's over at the fairgrounds exercising his trotting horses. Harness racing is very big in this part of the world, and so is basketball. Jock says you don't amount to anything in Harrison County unless you've got a trotting horse, a basketball, or a pickup truck. Well, you get the idea — I know everybody, and everybody knows me. That's what I like about Corydon. I'm not a native. I grew up in Indianapolis, but I had the good sense to marry a Corydon girl — Marydee was a Meyer — and settle down here and be happy. But I had to prove myself. These people are friendly, but they're Hoosiers — real Southern Indiana Hoosiers. They don't take newcomers for granted."

"Is that what Hoosier means?" I said.

"That's what it means to me," he said. "It's a strange term — nobody seems to know for sure where it came from. Except that it's of Southern Indiana origin, and goes back to our old capital days. The most commonly accepted derivation is that when a stranger knocked on a pioneer cabin, they didn't open up right away. They were suspicious. They called through the door 'Who's here?' But James Whitcomb Riley had a different explanation. He said it had to do with the Saturday-night drunken free-for-all fights where they gouged out eyes and bit off ears. Sometimes, he said, there would be a bitten-off ear left lying on the barroom floor. And the proprietor would call out 'Whose ear?'" There was a flash of white teeth in the dark of his beard. "How about another cup of coffee?" he said.

✦

We were sitting around a fireplace filled with greenery — Edward Runden and his wife, Linda, and I — drinking sherry and smelling the good smell of something roasting in the kitchen. Runden is forty years old, with an eager, boyish look and an inconspicuous mustache, and he teaches history at Corydon Central High School. Mrs. Runden, a vivid young woman with a fall of thick, dark hair, is also a teacher. She teaches behavioral science twice a week in a family-practice residency program at the University of Louisville Medical School. "Oh, sure," Runden was saying. "Randy West and I have a lot of things in common. For one thing, we both married local girls. Linda was a Keller. Her Cousin Bill runs the furniture factory."

Mrs. Runden smiled across the lip of her glass. "I'm also related to Art Funk," she said. "And to Fred Griffin's wife. And Bob O'Bannon. And Rosamond Sample."

"She's probably even some kin to Marydee West," Runden said. "Another thing about Randy and me — his first job when he came to Corydon was teaching at the high school." He took a sip of sherry. "And I used to be a newspaperman myself. That's how Linda and I met. That was in Chicago, at one of those demonstrations. Linda was demonstrating, and I was covering it for the Associated Press. I started out on a paper in Elgin, Illinois, and then I went with U.P.I. in Chicago, and then I tried the Foreign Service, in Iran, in Teheran, until our deadly foreign policy made me sick. I was glad to come back to Chicago. That's when I started working for the A.P. But by the time Linda and I got married we were both getting tired of city life — the ugliness, the squalor, the misery. So we got to thinking about Corydon. We subscribed to the *Democrat* — a terrific paper, by the way — to try to get the feel of the place. And, one way and another, we liked the feel we got."

"I liked the idea of connectedness," Mrs. Runden said. "And, I guess, the roots. My great-grandfather came here from Germany in eighteen forty-six. He arrived in New York, and the first person he met who spoke German was a black freedman, who was on his way west — on foot. My great-grandfather walked along with him and ended up in Harrison County. I think I miss big-city life more than Ed does. I seem to need people more. And then there's the conservatism here. Corydon must be one of the last places on earth where people in real need are too proud, too ashamed, to go on welfare. And you can imagine their position on something like abortion. Still, when I remember Chicago ..."

"Small-town life has its drawbacks," Runden said. "There is a certain lack of privacy, although people are aware of that and make an effort to keep their distance, to not be nosy. But lack of privacy doesn't bother me. It might if I had a Swiss bank account, or if I was into some kind of kinky sex. But I just don't have that much to hide. I think the good side of small-town life far outweighs the bad. If you have trouble with your dry cleaner in Chicago, he couldn't care less what you think or do. It's different here. You can't be ripped off. A person's reputation matters. And so does the individual. He can still influence the course of events. Corydon's still on a human scale. There's a sense of the seasons. There's a closeness to the basics. It's something to be able to hear a rooster crow these days. I think more and more people are coming to realize that. I think Linda and I are part of something interesting. We're in the first wave of people of our age and position who are moving away from the city — and not to the suburbs. Moving to the small town. To Corydon."

♦

There are a number of handsome houses of all ages in Corydon, and two of them — almost the oldest and one of the newest — are also, at least to local eyes, arresting. One of these is the McGrain House, of 1808 (now the home of Mr. and Mrs. Thomas D. McGrain), on its rolling riverside lawns. The other — an angular, thrusting, four-level cedar-and-glass example of the sculptured contemporary style which rises starkly from a hillside just above the McGrain House — is the home of Mrs. Rosamond O'Bannon Sample. I called on Mrs. Sample one day. "I don't think this house is all that strange," she told me. She is a small woman with green eyes and a cap of curly gray hair. "But it seems to offend some people. Not my father and mother — although I was a little afraid it would — and not my children. Not my friends — not my real friends, anyway. But the others! One of the nicer things they call it is 'that mine-shaft house.' I'm simply crazy about it. It's been very important to me. Building it helped see me through a very difficult time. My husband died in nineteen seventy-five. We had been living in my grandfather's old house, and after Bob's death I began to feel I wanted a change. I'm not a big historical person. I'm more interested in right now. I'm an artist, you know — I studied at the Traphagen School of Fashion in New York after college. I was brought up here, but I came back only because I wanted to marry Bob Sample. Well, one day I happened to open a copy of *House Beautiful*, and a picture jumped at me. I thought, Now, there's a house I'd like to build. I've always thought it would be wonderful to be an architect. So I took the picture to an architect — my friend Bob Applegate, in New Albany — and he drew some elevations, and I found a builder, and the three of us talked it all the way up. I loved every minute of it. I think I'd even like to build another — a *really* modern house. A geodesic dome, maybe, with solar heat. Then they'd really have something to talk about. I firmly believe that a house can be a work of art, of sculpture. We should *live* art. Corydon is my home, and I love it. The only difficult thing is being artistically alone. I miss the company of other artists. Thank God for Louisville. I show in the Louisville galleries and museums, and I have a lot of artist friends there. So — I don't know. I have my work. And I teach — this house, with all its light, is wonderful for that. I have my books. I suppose you know that we have a bookstore here in Corydon now. Which is just wonderful. They can get you anything. And I take almost every magazine there is — from *Architectural Digest* to *Rolling Stone*. And, of course, Corydon is *secure*. That means a lot when you're alone."

✦

Fred Griffin's car — his pickup truck — was parked on Beaver Street, across the street from his store, but before we reached it he touched my arm. "I want you to notice something," he said. "You'll notice that this side of the street is paved with brick. That's because this is where the hitching rack was in the old days, and the brick was there to keep the hitched horses from pawing up the dirt street. I'm sixty-three years old, and I can remember our old streets. I remember a sign they had on the hitching rack. It said, 'No Automobile Parking 8 A.M. to 6 P.M.

Reserved for Horses.' We had horse-and-buggies coming into town on Saturday right up to World War Two. This town had itself a good long sleep. No — that darn door is sprung or something. You have to give it a good hard slam. That's it! Now, maybe you're wondering why this street is called Beaver Street. All our other streets, almost, are named after trees. Well, the reason is there used to be a beaver pond along here in the old times. That's my house up there on the left, on East Walnut Street, right next to the Presbyterian Church. I'm like a lot of people here — I was born in the house I live in. Anyway, there used to be an open-air fur market back there on Beaver Street when I was growing up, and I remember getting up on Saturday morning and seeing the trappers gathering, and smelling the smell of the skunk skins. My Lord, that was a long time ago. I think I'll start our little tour with a sashay up to the old cemetery. There's something there I want to show you. But you might just look back when we get to the top of this hill. See what I mean? Our views are unexcelled. And it shows you what a hole we live in. I don't know why I call this the old cemetery. It's *the* cemetery. But this part here is the oldest part. And that headstone there is what I want to show you. It marks the grave of the only Confederate soldier buried in Corydon — the only identified grave. The poor fellow lying there was Private Greene Bottomer, of General Morgan's command. There's no point in getting out — the inscription's too worn to read very easy. The curious thing is that the marker was erected by a Confederate colonel named Bennett H. Young, who was president of the Louisville and Nashville Railroad, and who arranged to mark a number of Confederate graves in the area after the war.

"The next thing I want to show you is the site of the battle. It's out south of town, up beyond that knob on the left. We'll have to go back through the square, but it isn't too far. Besides, the fairgrounds is out that way. If only this was August, you could see some great harness racing. The hospital is out that way, too. And the new high school. A lot of land up there was the old Ashton farm. My wife is an Ashton. The battlefield is preserved as a nice little park. Harrison County has a park system we can really be proud of. If you look sharp off there to the right, you'll see Pilot Knob. Which is now a hundred-and-sixty-acre park called Hayswood Nature Reserve. It was a gift from the Hays family. So was the Battle of Corydon Memorial Park. This road we're riding on now is the old Mauckport Pike that Morgan and his men came riding up from the river. Of course, it didn't look like this then. Except for that big white house with all the trees. That's the old Hays homeplace. And here's the park. We're in luck: the gate's open. We won't have to get out and walk. Notice that old zigzag rail fence. You don't often see one these days, though we've still got a few around the county. They were the standard thing back there in eighteen sixty-three. They were what the Home Guard fought behind. The old-timers used to say the right way to lay a fence like that was to lay the bottom rails in the light of the moon. The pull of the moon was supposed to keep it from sinking into the ground. Or was it the *dark* of the moon? I'm darned if I can remember. Well, this is where they fought. I understand the battle lasted forty-five minutes. It was one of the very few Civil War battles fought in a northern state. That monument is interesting. As you can see, it's set so it faces north and south. The north face lists the casualties on the Union side and the south face lists the Confederate casualties. I want you to notice the trees, too. Some of those oaks were already here in eighteen sixty-three. If you want to read a good and authentic account of the battle, Art Funk has written a very interesting little book.

"Well, I guess we've seen enough of this. I've written a little book myself. It's called 'The Story of Indiana's Constitution Elm.' I'll give you a copy when we get back to the store. I wrote it a few years ago from notes that my dear old Aunt Jennie Griffin made. Aunt Jennie was chairman of the Elm Tree Committee of the Hoosier Elm Chapter of the D.A.R. I know you know about the Elm, and how it got its name and all that. But there's still more to it. All kinds of groups used to meet under that tree — from the Indians on up. It was so big and shady. It had a *spread* of one hundred and thirty-two feet. They tell me that even the Ku Klux Klan had meetings there. But there was never any kind of trouble. The Elm had a dignity that seemed to awe just everybody. Back in the early twenties, a couple from out of town drove up in an open-top touring car with a preacher aboard and got married under the Elm. But then it began to sicken, and it died in nineteen twenty-five. Well, something had to be done. They stripped off all the branches, and left just a fifteen-foot stump. Aunt Jennie recorded that thirty-four wagonloads of limbs were hauled off and sawed up and stored away all over town by the D.A.R. for souvenirs. Then they had a shelter built to preserve the stump. It was built of local sandstone, quarried just west of town, and it took one hundred tons to do the job. It's a beautiful piece of work, and that's what I've got in mind to show you next."

✦

"It usually works like this," Mrs. Jo Ann Kline, at the Star Cleaners, told me. "The tourists go to the Old Capitol and they hear about the Constitution Elm, and Christopher Tew, the curator, or somebody tells them that we have a full stock of relics, because this place used to be owned by a D.A.R. lady. So they come over here and pick out something to take back home with them. I guess we sell more gavels than anything else. They range from five dollars up to fifteen for the big ones. The

candelabra are the most expensive — thirty-two fifty a pair. The
letter holders and paperweights are nice. And then we have the
just plain pieces of polished wood. Oh, no — the proceeds all go
to the D.A.R. Of course, I wasn't around when it all began. I
wasn't even born in nineteen twenty-five. But they tell me it all
comes from the original Elm, and I believe them. So, yes —
they're guaranteed."

♦

"You couldn't exactly call our customers tourists," Paul
Conrad told me. He and his twin brother, Charles, own (with
their father) both Conrad & Sons Furniture and Conrad & Sons
Piano Company. "But they mostly are from out of town. Out
of town, out of county, even out of state. We're very strong in
the Louisville area. The Conrads have been in Harrison County
since the mid-nineteenth century. People like the idea that
we've been in business since eighteen ninety. They like that kind
of reliability. They also like the feeling of trading in a small
town. They think the small-town merchant is more honest,
more trustworthy — especially when you're buying something
expensive, like a piano or an organ. They think we have this
colloquialism."

♦

Corydon is the home of two thriving businesses whose names
are favorably known even farther afield than Louisville. One of
these, of course, is the Keller Manufacturing Company. The
other, which has the distinction of being one of just twenty-five
enterprises listed in the authoritative *American Glass Paperweights & Their Makers,* by Jean S. Melvin (Thos. Nelson, 1967),
is the Zimmerman Art Glass Company. The company is situated next door to the Arpac poultry-processing plant, on the
eastern outskirts of town, and occupies a corrugated-iron shed,
once painted a functional shade of green, that resembles a

crossroads garage. It is owned and entirely operated by two men — Joseph Zimmerman and Gene Baxley. Both are old Corydonians. "I don't know how it happens, down here where we are, but most of our customers are walk-ins," Baxley told me. "Around ninety percent. The rest are collectors from all over the country. I suppose the walk-ins hear about us from somebody up on the square. Our specialty is flowers opening up in bloom inside a clear crystal ball. All different sizes. We've made some that weighed as much as twelve pounds. We do morning glories, crocuses, roses, gardenias, pond lilies, and I don't know what all — anything we happen to think might be interesting to try to work out. Joe is the artist here. He learned to blow glass from his father, and I learned the little I know from him. We get good prices, but we have to. A good rose can take half a day. The big problem is getting good color. Many of the colors in this kind of work come from old colored glass. We melt it down and use it all over again. We've been lucky a couple of times. We got onto some old red railroad lantern globes up in Toledo — a beautiful color. Another time, we found some old blue globes down in New Orleans. We've got all the work we can handle. I shouldn't even be standing here talking to you. The week just isn't long enough for all the things we've got to do. Like make glass. Like get ideas and then blow the glass. Like keep the books. Like go hunting and fishing. And we've got to drink a little beer from time to time. We started this business in nineteen sixty-two, and we've been living happily ever since. The only trouble is, it makes me feel kind of guilty. I mean, anything as pleasurable as this has got to be wrong."

✦

"Basketball is king in Indiana," Jerry Conrad told me. Conrad, a tensely serious young man, six feet five and solidly built, is the basketball coach at Corydon Central High School, in Corydon. We were sitting on a bench in his office and workshop, the school gymnasium, where a banner strung across the ceiling proclaimed "Panthers Are Dynamite." It was late on a Friday afternoon, but two lanky boys were shooting baskets at the far end of the court. Conrad seemed to be watching them out of the corner of his eye. "Ohio is all football," he said. "Kentucky likes basketball, and, of course, they won the inter-collegiate championship last March. Still ..." He lifted his shoulders in a shrug. "But here in Indiana there isn't anything else. It's our heritage. Our kids start fooling around with a basketball at three or four. By the time they reach the third grade, they're into a regular basketball program at school. Some stay in and some don't — you've got to love the game to play it. Basketball has been very good to me. I grew up in Marengo, just north of here, and I'd probably still be there if it wasn't for basketball. It paid my way through four years of college — the University of Evansville. I had to learn the game. I didn't have natural ability. I was good, I guess, but not good enough. I mean, for pro. I played at college with Don Buse. He's with the Phoenix Suns now. I knew the difference the minute I saw him. I couldn't jump higher than two feet. Don had a lot of strength, very quick hands, and he could jump three feet. If you haven't got those abilities, forget it. Only a select few make it to pro. And it's getting tougher all the time. I've got a couple of kids here at school who could have got a basketball scholarship easy back in my day. They haven't got a chance today. People talk about the great black players. I've got a theory — at least for around here. The black kids really live the game. The white kids go driving around having a good time. The black kids mostly don't have a car. They stay home and shoot baskets. Basketball is a year-round game if you're going to play it well.

Just the season isn't enough. I keep the gym here open three nights a week all summer, and I'll get as many as thirty kids in here every night. Don't forget, this is Indiana. They say there are two best places to recruit college basketball players. One is the real big city — like New York or L.A. The other is almost anywhere in Indiana."

✦

Looking through the Corydon *Democrat* (three sections, forty-four pages) in Randy West's office one Wednesday (publication day), I came across a page headed "Harrison County Church Directory." The churches were listed alphabetically by denomination, and the listings occupied four columns. There were one hundred and four churches in all — Baptist, Catholic, Christian, Lutheran, Nazarene, Presbyterian, United Methodist, and Wesleyan, and such others as Bible Covenant, Full Gospel House of Prayer, Church of God of Prophecy, Trinity Church of Prayer, the True Church of God, St. John's Pentecostal, Kingdom Hall, Trinity Assembly of God. "That many?" West said. "Well, I'm not really surprised. Church is a big part of almost everybody's life around here. Our people take religion very seriously. They're sincere, God-fearing Christians. And very conservative. Fundamentalist."

✦

"Conservative isn't the word," the Reverend Elijah T. Perkins told me. Mr. Perkins was in his closing weeks as the pastor of the Old Capitol United Methodist Church — the largest church in Corydon — before moving on to a parish near Vincennes. He sat deep in his chair — a big, heavy man, with a big mustache, heavy horn-rimmed glasses, and a diamond ring on his finger. He shook his heavy head. "They're what I call mind-set. Do it our way or not at all. I'm new here. I was called here from Kentucky three years ago, and I'm not sure that I've adapted. There are a number of people in our congregation who aren't entirely pleased with the way I conduct our services. They think I'm too structured, too formal. They feel we must progress in the direction of more emotion. They want a celebration rather than formal worship. They want a chance to express their faith in a pentecostal manner — they want to experience the Holy Spirit in themselves. It disturbs them that I'm not charismatic, that I don't have the gift of tongues. There are ministers here who do. I'm thinking of my young friend Mark House. The fundamentalist churches are growing very rapidly. That may be the trend of the future. I acknowledge the power of prayer. I had asthma as a child, but at the age of twenty-one I prayed for help and my prayer was answered. God healed me. But anointing, laying on of hands, that's different. I was at a cottage service, a small group of us at a lady's home here. One of the ladies complained of some ailment. Our hostess was very concerned. She said she had some Oral Roberts oil, and she asked me to anoint our friend. I had to decline. And I'm afraid I dropped in their estimation."

✦

Mark House is the pastor of the Trinity Assembly of God Church. The Trinity Assembly of God is the newest church in Corydon, and House, at twenty-eight, is the youngest clergyman in town. I met him by appointment at his home. He stood at the door as I drove up — blue-eyed and smiling, booted and jeaned, vibrant with animation. He led me down to a basement office. "Praise the Lord," he told me. "My wife and I are very happy in Corydon. When we came here, a year ago, I found a congregation of ten people meeting in the old Masonic Lodge. We now have a congregation of about seventy-five, and with loans of sixty thousand dollars from the Corydon State Bank and our parishioners we've taken over the old Corydon

Baptist Church. I stand grateful to the Lord. I spent almost ten years in the wilderness. I grew up in New Albany, with an allowance of fifty dollars a week, and I went up to Indiana University in nineteen sixty-nine with clothes, a car, and all the credit cards. Those were the days of rhythm, riot, and revolution. I was a straight-A student, but the 'in' thing was to drop out, and I dropped out fast and far. I started doing drugs — pot, acid, and the psychedelics. I got separated from my dad. He didn't like the way I was going. No more allowance. I moved into heroin — using and selling. Everybody who does drugs sells. I was living at the other end of the barrel now. I was on the street. I made Atlanta, and Fort Lauderdale, and Chattanooga. I got busted. I was in and out of jail, I was in the Madison State Hospital, in Madison, Indiana. After four years, I made up with my dad. He was living in Chattanooga then, and I got a job driving a milk truck. I stayed straight for maybe six months. Then I went back on drugs, and got arrested again, and got put in a drug-rehabilitation center — on methadone. And that was the worst. Worse than heroin, more addictive. I'll say this right now — there's no solution to the drug problem but Christ. I got back to New Albany, and the second night I went out with two fellows to rob a doctor's office for drugs. But the doctor had an intercom, and he heard us and he was waiting there with a gun and opened up. One of us got hit. I never knew what happened to him. The other fellow gave up. They caught me four blocks away. They had me cold, because I had dropped a glove at the scene and the other glove was in my pocket. They told me I was lucky I wasn't lying there dead in the street. I sat in the jail that night and wished I was dead. I was so sick of my life.

"It's a strange thing. All those years when I was hitchhiking I kept getting picked up by preachers. I believe God was already dealing for me. I believe some angels intercepted those bullets

that robbery night. And after I'd been in jail a couple of days, a
man from the Christian Coffee House street ministry came in
and talked to us. He was only a boy — just nineteen. Some of the
men there made fun of him. They mocked him. I didn't do
anything. I was too busy having a pity party for myself. But he
came back again, and he sought me out. Praise the Lord! I'd
never had any church background. He began to share with me
— told me the plan of salvation. Ed Needham, that was his
name. And he asked me what I wanted out of life. I didn't have
to think it out. I said no more street scene, no more ripping off
and being ripped off. So he showed me Galatians 5:22: 'But the
fruit of the Spirit is love, joy, peace, long-suffering, gentleness,
goodness, faith.' And Ed said, 'This is what Christ said He
would give those who will live for Him.' It sounded tremendous. I'd been hard on the outside, but that outside was really
only brittle. God was able to break through. Ed asked did I
want to go to Heaven. Oh, yes! Then Ed said for me to ask Jesus
into my heart. I was ready to cry, but too proud. And all those
other prisoners were watching. I said, 'Lord, if you can do
anything with my life, you can have it.' But there was no
feeling of response — no angels, no neon lights. I said, 'I need
some methadone.' Then Ed's older friend, Bob, came over and
said he would pray for me. He laid hands on me and began
rebuking the Devil. He took authority over my sickness.
Something warm went through my body, and I was healed. It
shook me. I mean, to see God answering. He was concerned
with little old me.

"But I had been with the wrong team for too many years.
Some new guys came into jail and they had some pot. The old
Devil began talking to me. I started smoking pot again and
getting high and having a good old time there in jail. Then God
sent a guy back from the penal farm. He was living for God one

hundred percent. He showed me I was doing wrong. And the next day, when they said let's smoke some pot, I said no. I said I had decided to follow Jesus all the way. They kind of made fun of me. But I never had another experience with drugs. They made me a trusty there at the jail. I went across the street one day to the Floyd County public library to read about Jesus, and I got to talking to a girl there about Christ and my experience with drugs. She sat right back when I said I was in the jail. But she came to see me there. Her name was Theresa. And — praise the Lord! — Theresa is the girl who became my wife. About that time, the Lord came to me when I was praying and told me to go to the sheriff's office and confess everything I had done in Floyd County. I was confused. *Was* it God, or was it the Devil trying to trick me? I said to God that if He really meant it, to give me a sign. I got out my Bible, and it opened to Hebrews 13:6: 'The Lord is my helper, and I will not fear what man shall do unto me.' But the sheriff, when I told him what I wanted to do, he kind of backed off. Was I demented? I told him the Lord had dealt with my heart. The detectives there thought about it, and then they told me they thought I was sincere. They said they were going to put my record in the canceled-report file. That was early August of nineteen seventy-four, and they released me a few weeks later. I started going to the Assembly of God Church there in New Albany, and I got a job as janitor in the church, and Brother Drost, the pastor, practically adopted me, and I got in touch with Theresa, and she stopped smoking cigarettes and although she had been raised a Catholic, she came into the Assembly of God with me.

"I had been having trouble with my eyes for several years. The reason was drugs. A lawyer in Atlanta got me to a doctor. The doctor said it was retinal detachment, and he operated on my left eye to save it. But my vision in that eye was never better than wavy and blurred. But the Lord spoke to Brother Drost one day, and He told him to touch my eye. So he laid hands on me and we prayed. There was no obvious manifestation that night. But two months later, in church, a message came to me in other tongues. It was 'I am the Lord that healeth thee, and I am in the midst of my people and will work wonders tonight.' I heard it in my head, and it scared me so I couldn't stand up. But a man behind me got the same interpretation. I joined the healing line. I saw the shortened leg of a girl grow up to normal, and I burst out crying. I prayed to the Lord to heal my eye. And the next day I went to my ophthalmologist for a checkup, and he was blown away. I was seeing twenty-thirty. I was dating Theresa, and I was thinking, Should I marry her? So I asked the Lord. I reached in the little scripture box and took out a card. It said, 'I shall be satisfied.' So we got married, and the Lord called us up to the Teen Challenge unit in Muskegon, Michigan, to help kids fight their way out of drugs. We were there for fourteen months, and then the Lord spoke to us to go back home and start a church in a new place. He said, 'Take a conduit out from the Mother Church.' He meant Corydon. I wasn't ordained yet, but I was working for my ministry. I'll have my full license this winter. The ministry is not a job. It's a calling from the Lord, and I've been called. Praise the Lord! Corydon is a wonderful place. Our church is growing so fast. The average age of our congregation is between twenty-six and thirty-five. We have lots of kids. The teenagers are so open to the Gospel. They're hungry for the spirit world. The Assembly of God is the fastest-growing Protestant church in the world today. Our headquarters are in Springfield, Missouri. We fill a need. We preach divine healing. We believe in the gifts of the spirit — in insight. We believe in direct communication with the Lord. It is written in James 5:14–15: 'Is any sick among you?

Let him call for the elders of the church; and let them pray over him, anointing him with oil in the name of the Lord: And the prayer of faith shall save the sick, and the Lord shall raise him up.' Could anything be clearer than that? I know who I'm representing. Praise the Lord!"

♦

"Yes, well," Dr. Rashidul Islam told me. "We have seven doctors in the Corydon area, and we're all busy. We have a new, completely modern hospital, with sixty-eight beds and an intensive-care unit, and most of our beds are usually occupied. No — what concerns me is something else. I was trained in England, but I practiced in upstate New York and in New Jersey before I came here. I'm concerned with what I call the Small Town Disease. That's my term for obesity. It is especially a disease of the small-town woman. She marries young, right out of high school, and her life becomes centered entirely in the home, and the center of the home is the kitchen. She eats too much. She has no other outlet. She has no outside life except church and the high-school basketball game on Friday night. And she gets no exercise — she rides wherever she goes, even just down to the square. And the reason I call it the Small Town Disease is this: there is no social force in the small town to restrain her. I think of it as a cultural thing. There is no tradition of chic. The city woman responds to social pressures that she look well. The small-town woman doesn't care. Not in every case, of course, but most. She comes to me, and she's conspicuously overweight and headed for hypertension, and she says, 'I have to eat. It's my only pleasure.'"

Pella, Iowa

PELLA (population 7,800) sits islanded in the gently rolling cornfields and pastures of Marion County, in south-central Iowa, some forty miles southeast of Des Moines. As one approaches it (as I did) on the backwater highway from the south, it has the look of any prairie town — a cloud of leafy green billowing up across the open farmlands, a sudden thrust of grain elevators, of power-plant chimneys, of a water tower. The familiar continues — a Hy-Vee Food Store, an A. & W. fast-food drive-in, the Dutch Mill Motel, Don's Skelly Service, a Budweiser tavern with a window sign: "Mixed Drinks." There is a right-angle turn. Highway 163 becomes Main Street — becomes every other small-town Main Street: a long, long street of small clapboard houses, most of them white, with sidewalks and shade trees and porch swings and a letter carrier trudging along with his bag. But then the scene abruptly changes. A vista appears on the left. It opens, widens, becomes a parklike square: a good four acres of spreading maples and formal plantations of ornamental crabapple trees and flower beds and wagon-spoke walks and slatted green benches and a lily pond with a sculptured fountain. I slowed my car and looked. At one end of the square, lifting up from a spacious stylobate reached by two broad flights of shallow steps, were two great white columns surmounted by an elaboration of bells and rearing heraldic lions and a glittering golden crown. I followed the creep of traffic around the square. The business buildings that faced the square were narrow and brick-built, most of them of two floors, with stores on the street and apartments above. Many of them had stair-stepped gable roofs or balustraded roofs or mansard roofs or steeply pitched roofs finished with curved red tiles, and the façades of all but two or three of them were bright with intricate designs — painted, sculptured masonry or glazed ceramic tile. I found a parking slot near the soaring columns and got out. The sound of a carillon filled the air. I recognized the stately lilt of Offenbach's "Barcarolle." It seemed to come from the top of the columns. I stood and listened and stared. "I know what you mean," Dennis Friend, the news editor of the Pella weekly *Chronicle,* told me when I met him later that day. "I know exactly. I'm a newcomer here myself — from Omaha. I remember the day I arrived to take this job. My wife and I drove around the square. We looked at each other, and drove around again. And Konni shook her head and said, 'This isn't Iowa. This is Europe.'"

✦

Pella is not Europe, but it is, in certain conspicuous respects, European. It had its origin in the religious ferment that troubled mid-nineteenth-century Holland, and it still strongly reflects its roots. It was founded by a young dissenting minister of the authoritarian Dutch Reformed Church named Henry Peter Scholte and some seven hundred like-minded followers in 1847, and until well within living memory it was almost entirely Dutch. It is now merely predominantly (about ninety percent) Dutch. All the leading families of Pella are of Dutch ancestry, and many of them bear the names of the earliest settlers — Kuyper, Vander Voort, Vermeer, Gaass, De Vries, Van Gorp,

Dingeman, Lautenbach, Leydens, Van Zee, Bogaards. The Pella telephone directory lists seven Smiths and four Joneses. There are, in contrast, fifty-one Vermeers (or Ver Meers), forty-nine Van Zees, forty-five Van Wyks, and numerous Voses, Vrooms, Zylstras, Vander Ploegs, Steenhoeks, Stursmas, Roozebooms, Jaarsmas, De Jongs, Bruxvoorts, Bandstras, Nunnikhovens, Van Waardhuizens, and Gosselinks. (A ubiquitous bumper sticker in and around Pella asserts "Yer Not Mutch If Yer Not Dutch.") It is true that the mayor of Pella is an immigrant from Illinois named C. B. (Babe) Caldwell, but his wife was a Schakel, and he is the proprietor of Paardekooper's Drug Store.

The Dutchness of Pella is the natural legacy of its several vigorous founding families. The town itself, however, was (and to a large extent remains) the almost single-handed achievement of Henry Peter Scholte. Dominie (as he seems always to have been called) Scholte — born in Amsterdam in 1805, a graduate of the University of Leyden, and the recipient of a comfortable mercantile fortune — created Pella. It was he who chose Iowa as its site. (He is said to have first thought of settling in Missouri, but changed his mind when he learned that it was a slave state, and then, at the urging of a compatriot there, considered Michigan, before the rich and treeless prairie decided him on Iowa. "Not to detract from Michigan's fertility," he wrote with an appealing irony to his Michigan friend, "nor from the value of many kinds of wood, nor from the pleasure of hearing the warble of birds in the cool shade of virgin forests — I had, however, experienced enough of real life to know that stumps of trees are disagreeable obstacles to farmers, and that the value of wood decreases when everything is wood.") It was Scholte who bought, for cash, the land upon which Pella was built, and parceled it out at reasonable prices to his followers. It was he

who plotted Pella and (recalling the ancient Palestinian city of
Christian refuge) gave it its name. It was he who designed the
central square as Garden Square, and contributed the land for
another square of similar size, Market Square (now a park with
a bandstand). It was he who named the streets of Pella. The
original east-west streets honored the republican ideals of the
time (Liberty, Independence, Union) and the standard American heroes (Columbus, Washington, Franklin). The principal
north-south streets were less conventionally named. They designated what he conceived to be the ten stages through which a
Christian must pass to redemption: Entrance, Inquiry, Perse-
verance, Reformation, Gratitude, Experience, Patience, Con-
fidence, Expectation, and Accomplishment. (These names were
changed by a self-conscious city council shortly before the First
World War to conform to a more American tradition: Reformation Avenue, for example, became Main Street, and Gratitude became Broadway. Nevertheless, the old names have not
completely vanished from the scene. They are perpetuated at
the Pella Country Club, where they serve, not inappropriately,
as the names of the holes of its nine-hole golf course — all of
them but Accomplishment.) It was Scholte who brought a post
office to Pella, and he served as its first postmaster. He was a
founder and the first editor of the town's first newspaper, the
Gazette. He was, of course, the first pastor of the first church in
Pella. It was he whose gift of land (a city block for a campus,
and two farms to provide endowment) established, in 1853, the
still functioning and flourishing Central College of the Reformed Church in America. And on September 17, 1847, less
than a month after he and his followers arrived in Pella, Scholte
gathered his flock together on the site of the projected Garden
Square, where (as he recalled some years later in his memoirs)

"we made our first declaration to become citizens [of the United States], so as to identify ourselves as soon as possible with the land of our adoption." It was a declaration and an identification (proclaimed in Dutch by a company of men in wooden shoes and red shirts and black velvet jackets) that would seem to have forecast the future of Pella: a rejection of Holland, an ardent retention of everything Dutch.

✦

Pella, in the first year or two of its settlement, was a straggle of log shanties and cavelike huts roofed over with prairie-grass sod. Its Yankee Iowan neighbors called it Strawtown. The first permanent dwelling to be built in Pella was built for Scholte and his wife and three children, and it was built for permanency. Today, it occupies much of the block just north of the square. It is a handsome house, a freehand copy of a plantation house that Scholte had seen and admired in Missouri — a long, rambling white clapboard affair with galleries and bow windows and fanlights and much jigsaw ornamentation — and it is still by far the most imposing place in Pella.

Scholte's house is now the home of his great-granddaughter. Her name is Leonora Gaass Hettinga. Mrs. Hettinga is around sixty, a tall, attractive woman of disciplined poise and posture. I had tea with her one afternoon in her sunny Victorian parlor. "Oh, no," she told me. "I was born in the old Gaass house, but I've lived here most of my life. And, of course, I'm the last person who will ever live here. We've given the house to Pella — to the Historical Society. They plan to preserve it as a museum. And in many ways it *is* a museum. Almost everything you see here goes back to Dominie Scholte's time. You may have noticed that big iron chest near the window. Dominie Scholte brought his fortune to America in that chest, and it later served as the safe of the old Pella National Bank. The work of renovation has already started here. Martha Lautenbach, of the Society, and a couple of workmen are busy in the east wing right now. And Martha plans to furnish part of it from her family's collection of antiques. The arrangement is that I have this wing for the rest of my life. I couldn't ask for anything more. I love this house. It's such a beautiful house. An architect once told me that it could only have been built by a poet. I'm not sure I know what he meant, but Dominie Scholte did have taste, and he certainly built his house to last. The foundations are stone, and four feet thick. We made some changes in the plumbing a few years ago, and the workmen broke three jack-hammers trying to get through to the cellar. And the clapboard siding is walnut — solid black walnut. It's probably worth a fortune just as lumber. But there is sadness here, too. Dominie Scholte's young wife — lovely little Mareah Krantz — was never happy here. She was so young — only twenty-six when they left Holland — and she had been raised very gently and very elegantly in France. She was never cut out to be a pioneer. She may have traveled in a covered wagon, but she was wearing a blue silk dress that had been made for her in Paris, and a bonnet trimmed with flowers and lace. And she was attended by her personal maid, little Dirkie. There's a family story about their arrival here. They had all been traveling for days from the Mississippi River port at Keokuk. The wagon train came up from the Skunk River ford and stopped in this empty prairie. Dominie Scholte helped Mareah down from her seat. She looked around. 'But, Dominie,' she said, 'where is Pella?' 'My dear,' he told her, 'we are in the center of it.' I'm sure she tried to make the best of her lot. She had her children and her servants and her square piano and her beautiful Paris clothes and her twenty-three-room house. I've always admired her when they opened the barrels of lovely old delftware they had brought from Holland — and found almost everything smashed to smithereens. She simply gathered up the broken pieces and used them to pave a little garden walk. It's sunken away and vanished now, but I found a pretty little blue-and-white piece in the lawn one day when I was a young girl. Mareah lived here for forty-four years. She died in eighteen ninety-two, at the age of seventy-two, and she is buried beside Dominie Scholte in the family plot at Oakwood Cemetery. But her last words were 'I'm dying a stranger in a strange land.'"

♦

I drove out to Oakwood Cemetery one day toward the end of my visit and walked around looking for the Scholte family plot. It was a bleak experience. Most old cemeteries have a certain elegiac charm, a tranquility, a timelessness of dappling shade and sunlight. Dutch graveyard piety has an almost forlorn austerity. Oakwood has no woods — no oaks, no sheltering trees of any kind. I saw no flowers, not even in urns or vases, and only an occasional weedy shrub. I walked through ordered acres of almost identical headstones — little blocks of polished granite. Some were red, some were steely gray. There were no epitaphs. There were only names and dates. It had the chill of an actuarial file. I never found the Scholte plot.

♦

The president of the Pella Historical Society is a recently retired teacher of theatre arts and communications at Central College named Maurice Birdsall. Birdsall is a plump little man, and he lives alone with a little Boston bull named Doonie in a cluttered little house (circa 1853) on what was once Reformation Avenue, a couple of blocks from the square. I called on him one morning. "Well," he said, settling down in a throne-like chair in front of a smoldering fireplace fire. "I'll put it this way. I'm not a native, and with a name like mine — I mean, what could be more *English* than Birdsall! — I'm not even Dutch. But I am a Pellan: I've lived in Pella for over forty years — since nineteen thirty-eight — and I love it. I came here as a teacher, of course. Which was a most fortunate thing. I mean, I could never have made it as a businessman. This is a Dutch town, and in those days, before the Second World War, it was even Dutchier. I knew a couple — I won't mention their names, except to say they weren't Dutch — who came here from somewhere and opened a little business on the square. And the second day they were open a man came in — he was Dutch, of course — and advised them to sell out before they went broke. It was good advice, and they took it and left. Those were the days when if a Dutch boy or girl had a date with a boy or girl who wasn't Dutch it was a disgrace. It's different now. But there are still a lot of families who would feel real shame at a mixed marriage. Especially to a Catholic. Catholics — because of all those years of Spanish domination of Holland — are beyond the pale. As for the Dutch churches — the Reformed and the Christian Reformed — they seem to build a new one every year. I think the total now is sixteen. The congregations are constantly outgrowing the capacity of the buildings. I was raised a Methodist. But I like the Dutch. They're a very fine people. They have every virtue. Take that saying 'Dutch treat.' People think that that means the Dutch are stingy. Not at all. Actually, they are extremely generous. They're just not showoffs. They frown on check-grabbing. I love Dutch culture — Dutch antiques especially. As you can see, I'm a collector. Let me tell you about some of my nice things. I won't go into the furniture; it speaks for itself. But this little silver box. It's not a lady's compact, although I'll understand if you think it is. Actually, it's a Sunday peppermint box. In the old days here, all the way into the nineteen forties, the Sunday services were very long — an hour of prayer and a two-hour sermon. The ladies carried these little boxes of peppermint drops for the children if they began to get restless. I have another little box — Oh dear. Now, where did I put it? Well, no matter. It's a lovely little box the ladies carried for themselves. It held cotton soaked in cologne that they could sniff and revive themselves if they began to feel faint. Of course, the ladies were expected to sit quietly in their pews all through the service. The men had a masculine privilege. They could stand up and stretch."

Birdsall heaved on the arms of his chair and stood up. But it wasn't to stretch. He stepped to the fireplace. "My real collection," he said, "is my delft. This mantel, for example — it's faced in delft tile. Ah, I see you're surprised. You didn't know that delft could be *brown* and white. It can be many colors, although blue and white is, perhaps, the classic combination. Brown and white may have been the original delft. I know it was very popular circa sixteen sixty. They also made a beautiful polychrome. I'm afraid the best of my collection is on loan to the Historical Society Museum. That's just east of the square on Franklin Street — next door to the Wyatt Earp House. Oh, yes — we claim Wyatt Earp. He spent his boyhood here. But no matter. I'll put it this way. Delft is my passion. I wonder if you know that it wasn't even called delft until around the eighteen nineties. It began, of course, simply as chinoiserie — an imitation of Chinese porcelain. That would have been in the early seventeenth century. Delft was merely the name of the town where the best of it was made. This is interesting: Delft was originally a brewing center, but something happened and the breweries went broke, and to save themselves the owners turned to making this heavy glazed ware. There were seventeen factories there by the end of the seventeenth century. Then there was a shift in taste, and Meissen ware, or some call it Dresden, came into fashion. The Delft factories were out of business for many years. My delft is all old delft. Modern delft is entirely different. The color is no longer cooked into the clay. Some of it is very pretty. But I prefer my early delft. I wish I could tell you the value of my collection, but I dare not. I wouldn't want to tempt some vandal. Although, of course, there isn't much of that here in Pella. This isn't Des Moines. My only hope is that I can keep my collection intact and leave it to our museum. But you know about pensions in these days of inflation. And Doonie and I have to eat."

✦

Birdsall is not the only Pellan with a passion for delft. Delft of every kind — old delft, new delft, even imitation delft — is everywhere in Pella, and it appears in every form. Every home has its plates or pots or cups or bowls or trays or vases or pitchers or salt and pepper shakers or flower holders or figurines, or at least a decorative tile or two. The fronts of many of the buildings around the square are decorated with delft-tile panels, and so are many stores and offices and professional waiting rooms, and delft of every quality is sold in a dozen shops and stores, including, preeminently, the Jaarsma Bakery and the Vander Ploeg Bakery. "I almost started selling delft myself," Loren Vande Lune, the owner of the Central Park Café, told me. "I thought I'd have a little shop up front by the cashier's counter. That was a few years back, when I was doing this place over. I sent a big order off to Holland. But, you know, when my delft

arrived, it looked so pretty and nice I didn't have the heart.
That's my delft up there on those plate racks."

✦

Pella also has at least a developing passion for another form of
Dutch decorative art. This is a delicately mannered style of folk
painting that most typically involves formal bird and floral
motifs in soft shades of red and green, warm oranges and yellows, muted blues, dull whites, and charcoal grays. It is called —
from its place of origin, a port in Friesland — Hindeloopen
painting. The chief (if not the only) practitioner of the Hindeloopen style in Pella is a pretty blue-eyed blond woman of
forty named Sallie De Reus. Mrs. De Reus — Mrs. Darrell De
Reus — lives, and works, on a farm on the outskirts of town. "I
really owe everything to Maurice Birdsall," Mrs. De Reus told
me. "I studied art at Iowa State — the crafty side, I guess I
should say, like weaving and textile design and all that. But I
never found a real interest, a real direction for my kind of
talent, until Mr. B. happened to show me a book of Hindeloopen work. It was Dutch Hindeloopen work, of course.
Hindeloopen was never practiced here in Pella until I came
along. The early Dutch were opposed to ornamentation. They
never spent money on display. As I understand it, Hindeloopen
goes back to the eighteenth century, when there was a big trade
between the town of Hindeloopen and the Norwegian ports,
and the Hindeloopen traders began to bring back examples of a
Norwegian folk art called Rosemaling. Hindeloopen is an ad-
aptation of Rosemaling, with certain Indonesian influences,
especially in the stylized use of birds. It is and it isn't painting. I
mean, you don't frame it and hang it on the wall. It is essen-
tially a way of decorating furniture — chests, cabinets, chairs,
beds, all sorts of items. Like those louvred doors at the end of

this room. People bring me things to work on. Either that or I go out and work where they have something they want decorated. It's a rigid technique. Every design must fit the space, and it must maintain the tradition. But the brush technique can be very individual. My style is a little bolder than some I've seen. I've been very lucky. A lot of people are interested in my work. Dr. Overman, the optometrist on the Broadway side of the square, has four big panels on the front of his building. That was my first outdoor experiment, and the colors seem to be holding up very well. I've done a number of things for Ralph Jaarsma at his bakery, and for various people all around town. And I did the atrium at the Rolscreen factory. The commissions just keep coming in."

❖

Another Dutch art that is widely appreciated in Pella is the art of hearty eating. Most Pellans eat well, and the food they most prefer is heartily Dutch. There are three large and fully comprehensive supermarkets in Pella (and the usual mom-and-pop convenience grocery stores), but the Pellans also hungrily support two meat markets on the square — In't Veld Bologna, on Main Street (founded by Klaas In't Veld in 1939), and Ulrich's Pella Bologna, on Franklin — as well as the Jaarsma and the Vander Ploeg bakeries. I never once saw either of the bakeries or either of the meat markets without a customer or two, and in the late afternoon (and all day on Saturday) the bakeries were crowded three deep with skinny high-school students and taller, thicker Central College students and wide, matronly women with heavy-duty shopping bags buying apple bread, Dutch letters, lace cookies, pigs in the blanket, homemade egg noodles.

The Jaarsma Bakery occupies a two-story pink brick building of distinctively Dutch design on Franklin Street, a few doors down from Ulrich's. It is long and narrow, with a steep tiled roof and a high, stair-stepped gable front enlivened by a painted decorative panel — a red hourglass figure on a white ground — near the apex. The second-floor windows are hung with white lace curtains, and the display windows, with their tiers and trays of iced and sugared pastries, that flank the front door are trimmed with white lace valances. All the windows and the upper half of the door have leaded-glass panes, and there is a stained-glass fanlight over the door with the legend *"Brood En Banket Bakkerij."* "Well, *'brood'* means bread," Ralph Jaarsma told me. Jaarsma is forty-two years old, slight, smiling, and primly bespectacled. He and his brother, Howard, are co-owners of the bakery, but he is the manager and head baker. "And *'banket'* is pastry." I followed him through a doorway at the rear of the shop. We passed a table strewn with broken cookies and misshapen doughnuts, and skirted a gleaming fifty-pound block of almond paste that looked like a monstrous chunk of some semiprecious stone. We went up a flight of stairs to Jaarsma's office and a plate of cakes and cookies. "But that's about the extent of my Dutch," he said. "My Dutch is mostly bakery Dutch. Like *'kraklingen'* for figure eights, and *'krentenbrood'* for currant bread, and *'kletskoppen'* for lace cookies — things like that." He touched the edge of the cookie plate and pushed it a gentle inch my way. "Maybe you'd like to try one of our *kletskoppen*. They're one of the best things we do. Anyway, I got my Dutch from my father, and he got his from Grandpa. Grandpa was Dutch from Holland, and he founded this business. We started out in our house, working at home in the traditional way. Wood-heated ovens. Baking on brick. Everything made by hand. We did it that way until nineteen forty-seven. Grandpa even used to make St. Nicholas *speculaas* by hand. *Speculaas* are spiced cookies shaped like gingerbread men. I don't know how he stayed sane. We make the small ones now by machine. My father made the first changes. It was he who started our gift sideline of delft. Delft and Dutch silver and pewter and copper are an important part of our business now. Not as important as the bakery, of course, but they're a special hobby of mine. Still, aside from a modern plant, we haven't changed a great deal over the years. We still bake bread and make pastry that we can honestly be proud of. We sell our goods all over the state. A lot of the people you see in here on a Saturday have driven down from Des Moines. We still cool our bake room with fans. Air-conditioning just isn't practical there. And, of course, we still start baking at one o'clock in the morning. I've been getting a little lazy lately. I've got a good baker I can depend on, so I don't always come in these days before three o'clock. I can think of only two real changes since Grandpa's time. One is that most of our bread is now sold sliced. The other is that we are a little more American now in our pastry. We make it sweeter than they prefer in Europe."

✦

Robert Vander Linden — round-faced, pink-cheeked, tousle-haired — and I were sitting in his little balcony office at In't Veld Bologna on a rainy Thursday morning. In't Veld's is both a butcher shop and a coffee-break café. Below, beneath a high wire strung with foot-long rings of bologna, two butchers were at work behind a dogleg counter — sawing, chopping, slicing, trimming, pounding. There were customers waiting at the counter, watching every chop and slice, and three or four men, one of them in a business suit, drinking coffee at little tables up front. The walls were hung with colored photographs

of famous Holland windmills, and the display windows contained pyramids of quart jars of Maasdam's Famous Home
Made Pella Dutch Sorghum. "Yes, I'd say we're well established," Vander Linden told me. "This business is eight years
older than I am. I took over six years ago. I was born and raised
here in Pella, of course. One of my grandfathers came over with
old Scholte. But I was away for a while. I went to Drake, and
then I worked for the Nielsen survey people in Chicago. But
enough was enough. I'm not a born commuter. I prefer the
speed here. So I came back, and this opportunity turned up.
Pella has its drawbacks. Like Sunday. But there's a freedom, too.
I also like this business. I enjoy eating — maybe too much. And
I like what we sell. Bologna is a local specialty — Dutch bologna.
What it is is smoked, cooked beef sausage, with a very little
pork. Would you believe me if I said we sold between four and
five thousand rings of bologna every week? And the other
market does well, too. I have to prefer ours. The seasoning and
the quality of the meat are important factors. And the process.
Those are our secrets. How it's done is more important than
what's in it. Some people eat it as it comes. I prefer my bologna
cooked. I eat it every morning, boiled or fried, instead of ham,
with eggs. Our trade is mostly beef and pork. There's just no
demand for veal — except from the Weight Watcher people.
We have a few of those here — maybe we should have more —
and they come in sometimes and order ground veal. It's less fat
than beef, I guess. We sell a leg of lamb only every now and
then. Our staple here is beef and pork. Beef and beef bologna
and pork. Every kind of pork."

♦

"I've tried them all. I've raised everything, even sheep,"
Harold Van Zee told me. Van Zee, a large, bald, powerful man

in his sixties, is one of the biggest and most successful farmers in the Pella area. He and his son farm some three hundred and sixty acres of the rich black soil for which Iowa is famous. Most of it is in cornhog production. They market around two thousand hogs a year. "My opinion is that hogs are best. Pork is good eating. Is there anything better? And with some luck and a lot of work it can be profitable. But that isn't the point I'm trying to make. I *like* hogs. I like to be around them. They're different from cattle or sheep, or even horses. Hogs have personality. They're just as different as people. I've got thirty-two sows out there that I farrow. Some of them, I really love them. They've got the sweetest disposition. And there are some I just despise. I mean, there are some I want to pet and there are some I want to kick. You live with their natures for four to six weeks in the farrowing house and you get to know them. Some give me nothing but trouble. And I know why; I understand. They just naturally dislike me. We don't get along. But the others, the ones I love, they've got the sweetest dispositions of any females in the world. So which sows do I keep back to breed again after that first farrowing? I don't keep the ones that hate me. And when the time comes when I have to let my sweethearts go — when they've got too much age on them — why, it makes me kind of sad."

✦

I lodged in Pella at the Dutch Mill Motel, on the southern outskirts of town. I was comfortable there in a second-floor room (whose furnishings included both the usual Gideon Bible and a copy of "Reach Out: An Illustrated Edition of the Living New Testament, paraphrase by Ken Taylor, additional text by Harold Myra") with a view across the highway of one of Pella's many large and pleasant parks. But the Dutch Mill Motel has no café or coffee shop, and I took all my meals in town. I always had breakfast, and usually lunch, at the Central Park Café. The Central Park Café is agreeably Dutch in appearance (delft-blue façade, shuttered casement windows, much decorative delft tiling inside and out, and delft-blue booths and chairs) and also in much of its cuisine ("Our Specialty, Dutchman's Delight: Imported Holland Cheese Drizzled Over Hot Pella Bologna"), and its staff includes some of the prettiest, smilingest, most scatterbrained waitresses I have ever known: "Oh, gee, I'm sorry, I thought you said scrambled."

The Central Park Café opens at five o'clock in the morning and closes at ten at night, and Loren Vande Lune, the owner, seems himself to work that seventeen-hour day. I often saw him there in the late afternoon; he was usually there at lunch; and he was always around in the morning. I see him in memory — a vaguely troubled-looking man of around forty, thickly side-burned, heavily mustached — standing thoughtfully at the kitchen door, pacing the aisles between the booths and the tables, sitting with a group of coffee drinkers at a big, round table in the rear of the room. He sometimes sat down in my booth and sipped a cup of black coffee. One morning he joined me for breakfast. "This is late for me," he told me. "I'm the one who opens up, you know. I like to see that things get started right. I've got like a small army working for me. I've got fifty-five people on my payroll, including two Vietnamese and two Laotians. Those folks are about the hardest-working people I've ever seen. But, you know, I pull up out front at maybe ten minutes to five and there's always a bunch of people waiting there at the door. Construction workers, garbage collectors, farmers just come in to town, businessmen who just can't sleep. Last week, I had a cook on vacation, so I had to come in at four-thirty. But even then there was usually somebody waiting. I've learned to nap in a chair in my office. I don't know how much you know about Pella. Some towns have their high-class people and their low-class people, and the two don't ever get together. Pella is different. The well-to-do people here are humble people. The Bible group I belong to meets at the home of a millionaire. He and his wife are just plain people, and they have a nice, plain home. They like nice things. I mean, they like good food, and they have their cars and their private plane. But they don't show off. You wouldn't know he had a dime, to look at him, and his wife does all her own housework. And their kids work. I've had a lot of rich kids in here working waitress, even cooking. This is a democratic town — real Dutch democracy. Take that big table back there — those men sitting there drinking coffee. They're all kinds. They're businessmen and professional men and farmers and clerks and guys that work with their hands. Everybody here knows everybody else. And nobody tries to grab the check. They toss a coin to see who pays. The Bible says thou shall not gamble. I suppose you could call what they do gambling. But I look at it another way." He took a sip of his coffee. "I consider it a scientific method of determining who will commit an act of charity." Vande Lune looked at me, a smile formed, he broke into a throaty rumble. It was the only time I ever heard him laugh.

✦

"No, I'm sorry," Leonard Gosselink told me. Gosselink, another of Pella's many fourth-generation Pellans, owns and operates Gosselink's Book Shop, a few doors down from In't Veld Bologna, and the Main Street side of the square. "We don't carry secular books anymore. Not for a few years now. There just wasn't that much demand. You might try the Radio

Shack, over on Union Street. I understand they stock some
books. And, of course, there's the Carnegie-Viersen Public Library just across the square. Our book business now is all in the
Christian category — Christian living, marriage and family,
personal testimonials, devotional and inspirational, and Bible
study. It's the same with records. We specialize in Christian
contemporary music — what they call Christian rock and roll.
'Let's Just Praise the Lord,' by Bill and Gloria Gaither, is very
big. And so is B. J. Thomas's 'Happy Man.' Oh, you're welcome. Drop in any time. And God bless you."

✦

I dined my first night in Pella (on the recommendation of
Dennis Friend, of the *Chronicle*) at a restaurant called the
Strawtown Inn, and I ate there every night thereafter. Its name
recalls the sod-roofed shanties of pioneer Pella, but the name is
only a name. Strawtown is a thoroughly urban restaurant, and a
good one. It is situated on the western edge of town, three or
four blocks from the square, and is housed in a tall, narrow, red
brick building (circa 1855) built in the attractively functional
mid-nineteenth-century row-house style — an English basement, two full upper floors, and a dormer-windowed attic. The
attic at Strawtown is the bar (with Hindeloopen decorations by
Sallie De Reus). The two floors below, reached by a ladder-
steep stairway, constitute the restaurant proper, and the basement is a tavern (stone walls, exposed beams) called De Kelder
(or cellar), which offers a chophouse menu of steak, ribs, and
fried chicken, with a salad bar. Drinks are available, but most
De Kelder customers drink the house (jug) wine or, as everywhere in Pella, Heineken beer. The Strawtown is a formal
restaurant (fourteen-foot ceilings, white tablecloths and nap-
kins, candlelight, fresh flowers, reservations required), and its

three rooms together seat only a little more than a hundred persons. I had my first dinner at Strawtown at a front window table on the second floor in a delft-blue-and-white room, and I ordered from a delft-blue-and-white menu of heavy glazed stock. The listings were all in Dutch, but with English translations. There were fifteen entrées, among them *gevulde karbonade* (stuffed pork chop), *ossenhaas* (filet mignon), *wilde kip met paddestoelen* (Cornish hen stuffed with mushrooms), *Hollandse rollade* (Dutch spiced beef), and *Hollandse gebakken kip* (Dutch baked chicken with paprika). I had the chicken. My meal began with an appetizer of tiny meatballs in a spicy Indonesian sauce. Then came a cream-of-cauliflower soup. Then the chicken, served with a dressing of rice cooked with mushrooms and onions. With the chicken I had a half bottle of a nonvintage red Burgundy. There was a choice of apple bread or hard rolls. Then a salad of Bibb lettuce and tomatoes, with an oil-and-vinegar dressing. My dessert was *Hollandse kus:* vanilla ice cream with Dutch Advokaat liqueur. The coffee brought me back to earth. It was the standard watery café coffee of motel America.

The Strawtown Inn is the profitable enthusiasm of two of Pella's leading businessmen — Bob Klein, a manufacturer of work clothes, and Herman Stuart Kuyper, president of the Rolscreen Company, which makes Pella Windows and is the biggest industry in town. The inn is managed for them by a Mason City Iowan of Norwegian descent named Roger Olson. Olson is a tall, slim, unruffled man in his forties, with the effortlessly all-seeing eye of the experienced restaurateur. "My wife thinks we ought to change our name to Van Olson," he told me. "But I don't think that's going to be necessary. We've been here since nineteen seventy-six, and we seem to be fitting in pretty well. Of course, it helps to have people like Bob Klein and Stu Kuyper as sponsors. As I understand it, Strawtown was kind of an accident. This building here was standing empty, and the owner was going to sell it or knock it down and put up a store or something. Bob Klein heard about it, and he talked to Stu, and they decided it was a piece of local history that ought to be preserved. So they bought it. That was all for a while. Then Bob, and Stu's wife, Eunice, got the idea of turning it into a restaurant — a real restaurant, a restaurant that would do Pella proud. A landmark. They opened in nineteen seventy-four, and I jumped when I got a chance to take over. Nothing could be more satisfying than running the Strawtown Inn. Bob and Stu are businessmen, and they expect Strawtown to show a profit. But that's just a matter of principle. What they really want is quality. Quality is our maxim. We buy the best of everything. Iowa pork is the best in the world, and Iowa beef is as good as any, and so are Iowa chickens. We have a little trouble with produce. We have two good chefs and a good staff. We all take pride in what we're doing. We fill our dining rooms every night. I mean that literally. And we're just as busy in the dead of January as we are during the Tulip Festival, in May. Most restaurants, even good ones, like to get people in and fed and out. We do it just the other way. We want our patrons to enjoy the evening, and we encourage them to spend around two hours at the table. That was something of a problem at first. A lot of people around here weren't used to leisurely dining. They had to learn our pace. They had to learn to enjoy an apéritif, they had to learn to enjoy a glass of wine, they had to learn to linger over coffee. We don't emphasize our bar. It's there. It's the best-stocked bar in this part of the state. But this is a strict community — the Dutch drink, but they don't talk too much about it. We step very carefully. We have never advertised our bar. We only advertise the restaurant. But, of course, we draw from more than just the Pella area. We draw from a radius of around fifty miles. That includes Des Moines — we get a lot of people down here from Des Moines. And also from Ames. That's Iowa State, you know. And from Grinnell. You remember that storm we had the night before last? We had a party of four flying down from Omaha for dinner, but they couldn't take off; they had to cancel. I think we're successful in what we're trying to do. Our prices are reasonable for top quality in this part of the world. Eunice Kuyper put it very well, I thought, the other day. She said we were here to make a living, to make money, but money isn't everything. There are other kinds of profit, she said. We try to offer something of value to the community. We try to be a truly Christian business."

✦

"Well, the proper name — the Dutch name — is Tulpen Toren," Lloyd Vander Streek, the president of the Pella Park Commission, told me. We were standing at the foot of the double-columned monument that dominates the south end of the square. The carillon cleared its lofty throat. The melting opening chords of Schumann's "Träumerei" chimed gently down around us. Vander Streek raised his voice. "But everybody just calls it the Tulip Tower. It was designed by an architect named John Lautenbach. He did the original design in nineteen forty, and this is a reconstruction built in nineteen sixty-eight. It was a gift to Pella from Mr. and Mrs. Peter H. Kuyper, Stu's parents. You may have heard of Lautenbach. He was born and raised here, but he moved out East and made quite a reputation in New York. He came back here in the early fifties and built himself a home out in the country. He died a few years ago. I suppose the Tulip Tower does look a little strange to a newcomer. But his house is really strange. There's an inscription on the garden wall — well, I copied it down one day, and I brought it along to show you. Here's what it says: 'Erected to the Glory of God and Country with Prayers for the Ultimate Victory Over Malice, Scorn, Hatred, Envy, Criticism, Judgment, Bigotry, Prejudice, Intolerance, and Apartheid the Anti-Christ Found Lurking in the Church.' I'm not sure I really understand it. Lautenbach used to say he got the inspiration for the tower from the Bible — he likened the columns to the columns in the Temple of Solomon. What the tower is, of course, is the center of our annual Tulip Festival. That's held the second weekend in May — Thursday, Friday, and Saturday up to midnight. As you may know, we observe the Sabbath here. So the festival closes at midnight sharp. We don't even clean up until Monday morning. The festival includes parades, dancing in the streets, costume entertainments, and the crowning of a Tulip Queen. We can usually count on an attendance of around a hundred thousand. I own the Pella Bootery, across the street, you know, and I stock wooden shoes for the festival. You wouldn't believe how many pairs I sell. But the focus of the Tulip Festival is tulips. That's a large part of my job on the Park Commission. All the flower beds you see in all our parks are tulip beds. And our main streets are bordered with tulip beds. And most homeowners grow tulips. We estimate that we have in excess of a hundred thousand tulips in bloom at festival time. Oh, it's a wonderful, beautiful sight. Our bulbs are all imported from Holland. We plant about thirty thousand new bulbs every fall. You have to keep renewing the stock, weeding out the old, if you want to get big blooms. But the Dutch are thrifty, you know. We don't throw our old bulbs away. We give them away for home gardens. They do well enough there. Our colors are bright and cheerful: reds, yellows, pinks, whites. We avoid dark colors: the blacks, like Queen of the Night, and the purples — all those new inventions. They just don't make a good public display. Our tulips bloom for about a month. But, as I say, we Dutch are thrifty. Our flower beds don't sit empty. When the tulips are over, petunias go in. I think they're very beautiful, too. We have what you might call a petunia festival all summer long and into the fall. Now let's go back to the store. I want to fit you for a pair of wooden shoes. You'll be surprised how comfortable they are with a little piece of foam rubber at the instep."

✦

The reigning Tulip Queen at the time of my visit to Pella was a tall, willowy young woman of eighteen, with brown eyes and the light-brown hair that the Dutch call blond, named Mindy Roozeboom. "I don't suppose I'll ever get over it," Miss Roozeboom told me. "I traveled all over the state, I met the governor — so many things happened. There were thirty other candidates, and when the judges picked me I was just totally shocked. I think I know why they did, though. I wasn't the only pretty girl, and I wasn't the only girl with poise. But we each had to give a little talk about our most unforgettable experience. I told about my grandmother, who was a very valiant woman. She was a diabetic, and when I was just starting high school she had to have her leg amputated. But she didn't just sit back and give up. She had herself fitted with an artificial leg, and she was walking in no time. They say the Dutch are determined. Well, my grandmother was very Dutch. She used to say, 'You can do it if you try.' So I told about her, and when I came to her motto I said it the way she used to say it, in Dutch: *'Je kan het wel als je wil.'* I think that appealed to the judges. Anyway, they picked me, and I was just totally shocked. Totally. This has been such a great year — being Queen and all that, and starting at Central College, and I've even decided what I think I want to do. I want to get into fashion, something to do with textiles. So I hope to go to Iowa State. Of course, my parents don't approve. I have ten older brothers and sisters, and they are all living here in Pella. We're a close family, and Pella is home. But I don't know. I like Pella, it's a nice town, but — I mean, I've been living here for *eighteen years.*"

✦

Sunday in Pella is a difficult day for a visitor. The town observes the Sabbath with an almost Puritan rigidity. I arrived in Pella on a Tuesday, and just about everyone I talked with through the rest of the week told me — warned me — of its Sabbatarianism, but, even so, the reality took me by surprise. With certain humanitarian exceptions, no places of business — not even chain stores — are open on Sunday. It is generally considered reprehensible to wash one's car or mow one's lawn on Sunday. Pella has (by my count) ten service stations, but only one or two ("They're owned by out-of-towners," an attendant at Braafhart's Standard Service told me) are open on Sunday, largely to serve the traveler. The only eating place I found open for breakfast on Sunday was the Burger Barn. The Strawtown restaurant — but not De Kelder — opens for a couple of hours on Sunday for lunch (or noon dinner), but reservations are required two or three days in advance. The bar, however, is closed. The only place I could find to eat on Sunday night was George's Pizza, just off the square, on East Franklin Street. Most — perhaps almost all — Pellans observe the Sabbath in church, and many of these church-goers attend both morning and evening services. The only Sunday-morning sound in Pella is the sound of church bells, and the only stir of life is the bumper-to-bumper crawl of church-bound traffic. I spent the morning walking in the park across the way from the Dutch Mill Motel, and I had its eight or ten acres entirely to myself. In the afternoon, I drove down to the square, and my car was the only car parked on any of its streets. The square was as empty as the park. I strolled and sat on a bench and read the Des Moines Sunday *Register* for an hour or two, and in that time I counted three passing cars and a tractor-trailer truck. I found my way to George's Pizza around seven-thirty that evening, and I dined (soup, pizza, the usual transparent coffee) as leisurely as I could, along with a scattering of other Sunday strangers in town. It was almost eight-thirty when I gave up dawdling and finished, and as I stood at the cashier's counter paying my bill I saw a gathering surge of cars moving around the square. I walked up to the corner, to Paardekooper's darkened drugstore, and stopped and looked at the cars going by. There were sedans and pickup trucks and decorated vans and four-wheel-drive Scouts and Broncos, and the occupants were all young — a teenage driver and a girl. I marked a red Dodge pickup and watched it turn right off Main Street, move past the Solomonic Tulpen Toren, turn right again into Broadway. A couple of minutes later, I saw it coming south on Main Street. I watched it turn and move past the tower again. I stood there alone on the corner and watched the endless circling and recircling for fifteen or twenty minutes. I guessed there were at least a hundred cars involved in that obsessional parade. Once a boy in a gray Impala gave me a monkey smirk, and once a couple smiled and waved. I walked back down the block to my car. A couple were coming across the street, heading for George's, and I stopped them. I nodded toward the square. "What's going on up there?"

They turned and looked. They exchanged a glance. The woman laughed.

"You mean those kids?" the man said.

"Yes," I said. "What's it all about?"

"It don't mean anything," the man said. "It's just what the kids do after Sunday-evening church. It's like a custom."

"It's just something to do with your date," the woman said. "It's a way of showing off your girl. They call it 'Tooling the Square.'"

✦

Bob Van Hemert, the manager of the Pella Chamber of Commerce, tilted back in his chair in his big corner office in the yellow brick Wyatt Earp House. He is a big, comfortable man, with a big, smiling face. "Oh, the Dutch," he told me. "My grandmother was born in Holland, and Dutch was her only language. My parents both talked a lot of Dutch. I speak a little. I'm all Dutch, and I'm proud of it. I'm proud that this is a Dutch town. I'm proud of our Tulip Festival. I'm proud of our good Dutch cooking and the Dutch look of the square. And Dutch pride keeps this town as clean as any in the nation. But there's more to be said for Pella than just being Dutch — a whole lot more. I'm happy to be here to say it. Pella is a prosperous town. Our unemployment is practically nil. We have eight manufacturing plants here, and they employ almost half our population — thirty-three hundred men and women. Our pay rate compares favorably with any comparable community in this area. Clerks average three dollars and ten cents an hour. Machinists average six-twenty. Secretaries average four-thirty. Truck drivers average five-ten. Our biggest employer, of course, is Rolscreen. But we've also got Vermeer Manufacturing and Van Gorp. Business is good all over town. There's a waiting list for space on the square. You've seen our swimming pools and

parks and our hospital. Our industrialists are municipal bene-
factors. We needed a three-million-dollar addition to the hospital. The community raised the money in a matter of weeks.
And I'll tell you something else not many towns can match:
forty of our people — at least forty — are millionaires."

✦

"My father was a housepainter," John Hoogenakker told me.
"So were his father and his grandfather. So am I. That makes
me a fourth-generation painter here in Pella. I started work
back in nineteen thirty-seven. That was the Depression, don't
forget. But from that first day I went out to work I've never
had no slow time. I've never had a day off that I didn't take
myself."

✦

"I'd say John is one hundred percent correct," Edgar Roorda
told me. "I started my Pella Building and Supply company right
after I got back from World War Two, and I've never had to
lay a man off for lack of work. I've known a few who lacked
the desire to work. But that's different. There's money in this
town, and just about everybody has some of it. The average cost
of a new home now in Iowa is forty-five thousand dollars. The
average here in Pella is at least fifty-five thousand — maybe
close to sixty. And there's this: I've never had one of my houses
lost by the owner because he couldn't keep up the payments.
The people here in Pella know what they can afford. They
don't jump in over their head trying to impress the neighbors."

✦

"I guess I've worked for Rolscreen most of my working life,"
Henry Roozeboom told me. "Right now, my job is long-dis-
tance hauler. I've got children working there, too. Even Mindy
worked there last summer. They paid her four and a quarter an
hour for what she called putting screws in windows. Which is

not bad for a beginner — even if she is the Tulip Queen. Rolscreen is a good place to work. I get four weeks' paid vacation
every year. I get eleven holidays a year with pay — all the
regular ones plus Good Friday and my birthday. Everybody at
Rolscreen gets his birthday off. They give us life insurance,
dental insurance, Blue Cross and Blue Shield, and a Christmas
bonus. They also have a profit-sharing program. Everybody gets
about fifteen percent of his gross earnings every year. The average share is around two thousand dollars per person. But
there's more to it than that. Rolscreen is a nonunion shop.
Three times in the last fifteen years, the union has tried to
organize the plant. The first election went lopsided against it.
The second was a little closer. The third was more against the
union than the second. Why did we turn the union down?
Well, we listened to the organizers, and we thought a little bit,
and we did a little figuring, and it turned out that if we got the
union pay rate we'd all take a big cut in pay."

✦

I talked with Dr. Kenneth Weller, the president of Central
College, in his bright, book-filled office on the second floor of
Central Hall, the administration building, overlooking a
quadrangle campus with a long pond and a humpbacked Jap-
anese bridge. In the distance, I could see an avenue of flags
stretching in the breeze — the flags of Britain, France, Austria,
Spain, Mexico, and the United States. Students were standing in
groups or moving along the walks — the usual grubby, androg-
ynous students of everywhere. Downstairs in the lobby, I had
seen a wall plaque with a Zen-like truism: "Anyone can count
the number of seeds which come from an apple, but only God
knows the number of apples which can come from a seed." Dr.
Weller gave me a look of gleaming satisfaction. "No," he said.
"No, indeed. We are not a Bible college. We're much too old

and established for that. We're not even exactly a provincial college. Half our students spend part of their academic life studying abroad, in one of the several countries where we have an arrangement. Those flags represent our foreign connections. The fact is, we require only one course in religion. No, what we are is a Christian college in the philosophical or ethical sense. We're not interested in doctrine. Our basic tone is a concern for values. We're weak on piety and strong on life in its wholeness. We're concerned with how things work, but also with what ought to be. We remember here that Watergate was not the work of uneducated people. It was the work of highly educated people deficient in morality and ethical sense. We attempt to teach that ethical sense — to reestablish it, I should say. To that extent, we're concerned with the total lives of our students. Pella has always been an appropriate setting for our work."

A bell rang. A couple — a boy and a girl? two boys? two girls? — ran hand in hand across the bridge. Dr. Weller had his back to the window. He straightened a file of papers on his desk. "Last Monday," he said, "we had a young male student killed in an auto accident. His friends organized a memorial service. It was spontaneous. There were Scripture readings and readings of secular poetry. Four hundred people attended. Our enrollment is fifteen hundred. We have a sense of community here, and I think that that turnout is a good demonstration of it. We think of it as a Christian sense of community. And it isn't just here at Central College. It embraces the whole of Pella — the college, the churches, the business community, everybody. It *is* the whole of Pella. Even newcomers here seem to feel it. I know I did. I'm Dutch myself, but I'm from Michigan, and I've been here only since nineteen sixty-nine. There is a pervading community sense of heritage — an almost mystic feeling of roots. And roots are a source of community. Responsibility equates with community. You see this responsibility, this morality, this ethic in the personal frugality here and the public generosity. I'm sure you've heard about the generosity of our industries. But they aren't the only givers. Everyone gives to his capacity. Even the plainest people give. It's something that goes much deeper than the more conspicuous pieties — deeper than the Sabbath and all that. It's the real thing." He touched the file of papers again. "Now, don't misunderstand me. I'm not saying that we're unique — that we're an oasis here in the middle of the twentieth century." He stopped. He sat smiling at me across his desk. His smile faded. He shrugged. "No," he said. "I'll amend that. We *are* a little oasis here. I'm afraid that's exactly what we are."

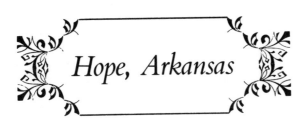

Hope, Arkansas

I SPENT the better part of a month in deep southwestern Arkansas — in Hope (pop. 10,290), the seat of Hempstead County — and the sun shone every day of my stay but one, and the nights were mild, and many of them were moonlit, and almost every night I fell asleep to the long, slow, faraway whistle of a freight train. I arrived in mid-March, in the first full rush of spring, and the day I left, in the second week of April, the pell-mell Southern spring was over and the endless Southern summer had begun. I saw the jonquils bloom and fade, and the azaleas and the yellow bells and the tulip trees, the wisteria and the redbuds, the peach trees and the apples, and I watched the big willow oaks that line the streets burst almost visibly into shading leaf. Only the glory of the magnolias — and there are magnolias in every yard and park and cemetery in Hope — was yet to come.

✦

Hempstead County is a gently rolling countryside of fields and woods and brushy creeks. I have never seen a countryside more pleasing. There is a creek in every hollow, and there are tall stands of hickory and loblolly pine on every slope and hilltop. The fields were once all cotton fields (Hempstead County long-staple cotton for many years was quoted as a premium cotton on the Liverpool Cotton Exchange), but that was a generation or more ago, before synthetic fiber. There are no more cotton fields in Hempstead County. Its agriculture now is watermelons and peaches, pecans and rice, soybeans and beef cattle, table eggs and broiler chickens. Especially chickens. Arkansas is the leading producer of broilers in the United States, and Hempstead County (with an annual production of around forty million birds) ranks among its most productive counties. "Oh, my, yes," C. M. (Pod) Rogers, Jr., circulation director of the Hope *Star*, told me. "And we eat it, too. We love chicken here in Hope. We've got Colonel Sanders and Chicken Country both, and there isn't a restaurant in town, except maybe El Matador, that doesn't specialize in deep-fried chicken. I sometimes eat chicken for breakfast, dinner, *and* supper. One night, I said to my wife, 'Let's just take the mattress off the bed and roost on the bedpost.' " Hempstead County also has a flourishing subagriculture: like many other Arkansas counties, it is legally dry, and deep in its briary woods and remote creek bottoms are an untold number of moonshine-whiskey stills.

Hope is situated on a stretch of tabletop prairie at about the center of the county. It has little of the beauty of the surrounding countryside. It is a comfortable town, generally clean and mostly well kept, but plain — not unattractive, just plain and unassertive. It is moderately prosperous and steadily growing. Its population increased by almost fifteen hundred between the 1970 and the 1980 censuses. It has forty-two churches (all but one of them Protestant, and almost all of those Baptist), twenty-seven grocery stores, twenty-two places to eat (most of them fast-food drive-ins), seventeen beauty parlors, twelve lawyers, ten doctors (including an osteopath and a chiropractor), nine pharmacies, seven furniture stores, three gun shops (for whose customers Jack's News Stand & Recreation Room carries a selection of sympathetic periodicals: *Gun News,*

Gun Times, Gun Journal, Guns, Gun World, Guns & Rifles, Guns & Combat, Guns & Ammo, Combat Handgun, Shooting, and *.44 Mag Power*), four banks, and Lee's Christian Book Store. Hope is in many ways an enterprising town and, in a very real sense, a democratic town. There is hardly a residential block without at least one substantial house, and there are very few blocks without a run-down, weed-grown nineteen twenties bungalow. There are many curious contrasts, some of them only too visible. Hope has an eighty-acre city park, with a swimming pool (fully and painlessly integrated) and tennis courts and baseball fields and hiking trails and a convention hall and a livestock-auction barn and a fairgrounds, and adjoining it are several blocks of new, well-built, fully integrated low-cost housing. But its only hospital is antiquated beyond the point of renovation, and across the street from City Hall and its parklike grounds is a tumble-down mansion that is a veritable hobo jungle. The hub of the business district (the intersection of South Main Street and Second Street) is prettily graced by a little islanded plaza, with benches and shiny live oaks and planters of flowering shrubs and a geysering ornamental fountain — a Housing and Urban Development project, built in 1976. Around the corner, on the wide sidewall of a three-story building, is a painted advertisement, its letters faded but legible from up to two blocks away: "Delicious and Refreshing — Drink Coca-Cola — Relieves Fatigue — Sold Everywhere — 5¢." The two most imposing buildings in Hope are the National Building and the First Baptist Church, and they stand a block apart on Main Street. The First Baptist Church — red brick with white trim and a soaring golden steeple — embraces (with its wings and annexes and lawns and parking lot) most of a city block. The National Building, a four-story office building faced with white marble and equipped with one of the two elevators in town, stands empty, boarded up, a derelict. Idlers on the benches in the plaza in the morning sit in its spectral shadow.

Hope is and has always been a railroad town. It is served by the main line of the Missouri Pacific, by a branch line of the Louisiana & Arkansas, and by a branch line of the Frisco. It was, in fact, a railroad stop before it became a town. Its progenitor was the Cairo (Illinois) & Fulton (Arkansas) Railroad Company. Fulton, on the Red River, a tributary of the Mississippi, in southernmost Hempstead County, is now a hamlet of about three hundred people but was then a busy port. The tracks of the Cairo & Fulton, moving south and west from Cairo, reached the naturally graded prairie now occupied by Hope in July of 1873. A depot was erected there to mark the line's momentary terminus, and the company's land commissioner — one James M. Loughborough — was inspired to distinguish the terminus with a name. The name he chose was the name that he and his wife had chosen for their daughter. About a month later, on August 28, the Cairo & Fulton — by then abruptly metamorphosed into the more ambitious St. Louis, Iron Mountain & Southern Railroad — decided that Hope had a future as a town, and offered lots for sale. (Ten years later, local records show, it *was* a town, of two thousand.) The railroad company also laid out the town streets. With much the same economy of imagination that Loughborough had used in naming the town, the railroad named its streets, designating the street paralleling the tracks Division Street and its principal intersecting street Main Street. The streets paralleling Division on the north were named for the letters of the alphabet, those on the south were numbered (beginning with Second Street), and those flanking Main Street were named for the trees that came most readily to the nineteenth-century mind: Spruce,

Laurel, Hazel, Walnut, Elm, Vine, and Pine. In 1908, Vine Street was renamed Louisiana Street, to celebrate the coincidental arrival of the Louisiana & Arkansas and the Frisco.

Hope is not only a railroad town but an active railroad town. It sees — and hears — the daily passage of some forty freight trains and (at the time of my visit) two Amtrak passenger trains. ("Business?" Clarence Adams, the Missouri Pacific agent in Hope, said to me. "Oh, hell, it's *good*. Last year, we were at the top in the country in terms of return on investment. And business should be good. What makes me laugh is the trucking lobby. A freight train can pull a lot of freight. I mean, one freight car can carry the load of at least four eighteen-wheelers. If all the stuff the railroads carry was put on trucks, I'll tell you this: you wouldn't be able to even get on the ramp to the highway.") Hope is also — since the Missouri Pacific tracks run roughly east and west through the center of town, and those of the Louisiana & Arkansas and the Frisco run roughly north and south — a town of numerous railroad crossings. At some point, almost every street intersects a railroad track, and at some time every day almost every resident of Hope is halted at a crossing by a passing train. The Amtrak trains are short (six or eight cars) and fast, but the freights move slowly and at length. Harry Shiver, the chief local historian, who lives on the north side of town, has noted in a recent memoir, "I . . . probably have spent a month of my life waiting to get across the tracks." When I arrived in Hope, I spent the first ten minutes of my visit waiting in line at the Hazel Street crossing for four Missouri Pacific locomotives, a hundred and twenty-five freight cars, and a caboose to creep, clanking and clamoring, past. I waited that first time with some impatience (although it gave me my first look at the "5¢ Coca-Cola" sign), but I later learned to almost enjoy such interludes. I became familiar over the days and weeks with a diverting roll call of strange or forgotten railroads: Maryland & Pennsylvania; Alabama State Docks, Port of Mobile; Cotton Belt; Marinette, Tomahawk & Western; Soo Line; Boston & Maine; Ashley, Drew & Northern; Seaboard Coast Line; Katy; Louisville & Nashville; Moscow, Camden & San Augustine. "I practically live on the Missouri Pacific tracks," Billy Burton, managing editor of the Hope *Star*, told me. "Our house is at the corner of Spruce and Division. When Melissa and I first moved there, the trains used to rattle us out of bed at night, but now they're a lullaby. They rock us to sleep. The quiet sounds louder than the trains. Melissa is home most of the time, and she's got so she can identify all kinds of different train whistles. And our fourteen-month-old baby's first words were 'choo-choo.' "

✦

I stayed in Hope at the Hope Quality Inn, two miles northwest of town (and of the Missouri Pacific tracks), in a big new room on the second floor, with a big window that gave on a wild-flower meadow and a distant wall of greening woods. I ate my breakfast in the restaurant there, and most of my dinners. I lunched in town, sometimes at El Matador and sometimes at Dub's Country Bar-B-Q, and often at the Crescent Drug, just off the plaza. The Crescent Drug — cool and dim and faintly scented with some reminiscent scent — is an anachronism, a survivor, a (to me) beguiling relic of the long-gone days when the corner drugstore was a social center and its heart and soul was its gleaming marble soda fountain. I had my first lunch there and my last, and my lunch was a local favorite, a sausage patty between two halves of a hot biscuit, and my drink was the table wine of the region, iced tea.

Early in my stay at Hope, I asked an acquaintance where the

best place to eat was. She thought a moment, and said, "At home." And, indeed, the best meal I had in Hope *was* at home — at the home of Billy and Melissa Burton. But I had many good meals at the Quality Inn. Breakfast there was both good (as it almost always is in the South) and cheap. There were many club breakfasts on the menu — two eggs with biscuits and gravy, one egg with sausage and biscuits, two buttermilk pancakes with bacon — priced at $1.49. Grits or hashed-brown potatoes, extra. Meat is preeminent in Hope. (At breakfast one morning, when I ordered only orange juice, a sweet roll, and coffee, the waitress said, "No *meat?*") Not all meats, however, are available. "No, sir," the butcher at the Safeway Store told me. "We don't carry veal or any kind of lamb. Folks here just won't eat it." He waved a hand along the meat counter. "That there's what they eat." I walked the length of the display: beef, pork, chicken, catfish, and some oddities — pork ears, pork neck bones, pork tails, hog maws, turkey necks, turkey tails. Beef (the heavy beef of the Southwest), in the form of pot roast or rib-eye steak or chicken-fried steak, was always on the menu at the Quality Inn, and so were roast pork and pork chops and ham. Ham was served with cornbread and mashed sweet potatoes topped with toasted marshmallows. Twice a week, on Friday and Saturday nights, there was a special seafood buffet, an all-you-can-eat groaning board of deep-fried catfish, deep-fried frog legs, deep-fried shrimp, shrimp creole, shrimp jambalaya, and boiled shrimp, along with French-fried eggplant and zucchini casserole, rice and hush puppies, head-lettuce salad, and Jell-O. Those evenings were also enlivened by a pianist named Charles Bostain with a constant and pleasing repertoire of pre-1940 blues and, at least once every hour, a joyous, strutting, stomping "Dixie." Fried chicken — crusty pieces the size of a fist — was available at every meal but breakfast. Hearty eaters at breakfast ordered chicken-fried steak, usually with two fried eggs on top.

✦

I came down to breakfast one morning, and a pretty, round-faced, blue-eyed, blond-haired girl at the front desk — a new face to me — gave me a wide good-morning smile. I said it looked like another beautiful day.

"I don't know," she said, and shook her head. "They're hollerin' rain."

✦

The first person I met in Hope was a tall, poised, immaculately dressed man of middle age named Hulan White. White is the principal owner of Herbert Burns, Inc., the principal men's-clothing store in Hope, and it was he, stepping out on the sidewalk in front of his store and heading me toward the plaza, who directed me to the serenity of the Crescent Drug. "I think people are beginning to change their minds about Arkansas," he told me in one of our several talks. "They're beginning to see us as we are — a beautiful state just waiting to be discovered. We're not all barefooted hillbillies settin' on the front porch and spittin' tobacco juice. We're the Sun Belt now. We've got more new people coming into town than you would believe possible. A couple came through here and saw our big Watermelon Festival, and went back home to Virginia and sold out and moved to Hope. And I don't reckon on it was just because they liked watermelon. That's how we got Klipsch and Associates, the big loudspeaker-systems people. Paul Klipsch saw Hope when he was an Army officer during the Second World War, and he liked it and decided that it was the place for his plant when the war was over. Our big chicken industry was started in the same way — by a woman from Illinois who was passing through. And I'm not talking only about white people. A lot of our new people are black. They like Hope. We have a big black population here — thirty-five or forty percent. It's been a long time since we've had any kind of race trouble. Our schools were integrated as smooth as silk. We've got black people working in our stores, and even in the banks. I sell them their Sunday suits. I'm not trying to pretend that the whites don't still have the advantage here. I don't know of any place where they don't. But things have improved for the blacks. A lot of people tell me the problem is worse up North."

"You *know* I'm a newcomer here," Mrs. Gayle Emis told me. "All I have to do is open my mouth." Mrs. Emis is one of the front-office staff at the Quality Inn — a trim young woman full of bounce and banter — and she and her husband, Donald, a trucker, moved to Hope in 1978 from Southern California. "Originally, though, we're from the Chicago area. We tried the Coast, and then we lost our four-day-old baby and that changed everything. We wanted out of there, and we started looking at maps, and when we came to the Arkansas map we saw the name Hope. It sounded so right, so hopeful. We wrote to the Chamber of Commerce, and they were great. They told us everything we wanted to know, and that settled it. We came here, and it was the best move we ever made. The people are all so darned friendly, and we were lucky enough to find a nice house on an acre of land, and we have a garden and everything. We just love Hope: the size of it — Little Rock seems so big to me now it scares me — and the peace and quiet. Last year at the Watermelon Festival, I even had my picture taken with the Arkansas Poultry Princess. I only wish one thing. I wish they had a cocktail lounge here."

"Well, yes," Mrs. Mickey Becherer (pronounced "Beacher") told me. "I guess you could say that we're newcomers to Hope."

Mrs. Becherer, a plump, animated woman with a pompadour of thick gray hair, and her husband, Terry, own and operate Becherer's Jewelry Store, on South Main Street, across from the Crescent Drug. "At least, my husband is. I grew up here and went to high school here, and even worked in this store when it was called Stewart's. But I left in nineteen forty-eight to get married, and we lived in Maryland until Terry retired and the Stewarts invited us to come back and take over. I was tickled to death. Hope is a *nice* town. People care about you here. Sometimes even to the point of being nosy. When somebody gets sick or dies, the neighbors all pitch in and help. They bring in food you wouldn't believe — casseroles, cakes, green beans, a ham. There's a pace here that I like. It's so different from the East. Hope is just a nice old country town. And if you had come in to talk to me a week ago instead of today, I would probably have said it was the kind of place where nothing ever happens.

"But that was before last Monday. I was alone in the store that morning and this well-dressed little colored girl came in. She was cute as a button. She bought a pair of gold earrings — good earrings — for forty-five dollars. Then she started talking. She was from St. Louis. We sure had a nice store here. Did I always keep these cases locked? How much was this? How much was that? What about those men's diamond rings? Did we repair watches? Good, because she had a watch that needed fixing. And she left it with me. That was that. Until I came back from lunch, just after one o'clock, and Terry went out, and I was alone in the store again. The door opened, and that cute little girl walked in with two nice-looking, well-dressed colored men. She said there wouldn't be time to have her watch fixed here. So I got it and gave it back. Then she said to one of the men, 'Here's those rings I was telling you about.' And they asked if they could see some. I took out four rings — the most we ever show at one time. That's when the game began. It was a real cat-and-mouse game. Everybody moving around and talking at once. Could I see that? How about that one there? Can I take this up to the light? Did I have any good cigarette lighters? I knew what was happening, but there wasn't a thing I could do. I couldn't get to a phone. Oh, they were clever. It was as good as a show. Then all of a sudden the store began to fill up with other customers, and the next thing I knew the girl and her friends were gone. And I was missing two men's diamond rings worth two thousand dollars. And they were such nice-looking people."

✦

It was an endless Sunday afternoon, and I was leaning on the high wooden counter at Police Headquarters, in City Hall, talking with the dispatcher. "Sure, we have some crime here," he told me. "We're getting a lot of amateur burglaries, and I wouldn't leave my car unlocked with anything of value on the seat. Once in a while we raid a still. And every now and then we get a murder, but it's almost always what I call a crime of passion. A couple of guys. Or a guy and his girl. And they're usually both of them drunk."

His telephone rang. I watched him listen, ask a question, give some instructions, but it was all a mumble to me. He hung up, and dialed a number. More talk. He turned back to me. "Fellow got fired at the Texaco station yesterday," he said. "Mean ole guy, they say. Now we've got a report that his car is parked at the station. Which is closed on Sunday. And the door of the office is open. The owners say he's got no business there. We've got a patrol car moving in. So we'll wait and see."

I waited, and got tired of waiting, and left. A few hours later, at the Pizza Hut, I saw the dispatcher at one of the tables.

"Oh," he said. "How you doing? Well, you didn't miss

anything. We found the guy in the station. He still had his key. He'd been drinking beer, and he was in the rest room."

✦

The mayor of Hope is a calm, casual, rosy-cheeked forty-year-old man named William E. Butler. He is also, and more gainfully, employed as president of the First Federal Savings & Loan Association of Hope. "There's a trend these days toward thinking that what's good for business is good for Arkansas," Butler told me, tilting back in a big upholstered chair in his big glass office at the bank. "Well, I don't agree. Very few of us around here do. This is still an unspoiled state, and Hope is an unspoiled town. We like it that way. We have a sound agricultural base. And we have a good industrial base — a healthy, diversified industry. It's clean and pleasant. It accepts the environment. It doesn't pollute the air or the soil or the water, or even the eye. We live within our municipal budget come hell or high water. We've saved our downtown business district. We've made it more workable, with parking lots and the way the traffic flows around the plaza, and more attractive, with those vapor lights and sidewalk plantings. We're handling the race problem as well as anybody. Floyd Young, our vice-mayor and one of our seven city councilmen, is black, and he's no token. Neither is Vander Lloyd, the assistant executive director of the Hope Housing Authority. I wish we could get rid of that dang Prohibition. It's an economic loss. And all it means is that they have to drive thirty miles down to Texarkana. And a lot of them never make it back in one piece."

✦

"I'm a Presbyterian," Vincent W. Foster, founder and president of the Foster Realty Company, told me. "I believe in taking a drink. And, of course, I agree with Bill Butler about Prohibition. But I don't have to go all the way down to Texarkana unless I happen to feel like taking a drive. All I got to do is pick up that phone over there and dial a certain number. And I'm not talking about moonshine."

✦

Vice-Mayor Young, like Mayor Butler, has a second, and more remunerative, job. He is assistant director and guidance counsellor at the Red River Vocational Technical School, on the southern outskirts of town. He is also a director of the Hope-Hempstead County Chamber of Commerce, vice-president of the Kiwanis Club, vice-chairman of the Arkansas Teacher Retirement System, and a member of the board of the Southwest Arkansas Planning and Development District. And a few days after I arrived in Hope he became the 1981 Citizen of the Year of the Hope-Hempstead County Chamber of Commerce — the first black man so honored. "I was at the banquet," Mrs. Bonnie Routon, the wife of a Hempstead County farmer, and the publisher of an elegantly printed local quarterly called *Hope Tracks*, told me. "And I never saw anything like it in my life. The Citizen of the Year is always a well-kept secret, and when Paul Henley called out Floyd Young's name the whole crowd just stood up and roared. There must have been eight hundred people there. And they all stood up and cheered — except, of course, a little handful of diehards."

"It sure was a well-kept secret from me," Young told me. "I was really surprised. I didn't know if I was going to be able to handle it. But I had my wife and family with me, and it was a long walk down there to the stage, and that gave me time to take hold of myself." We were sitting in his office at the Red River School. He looked at me across his desk — a solid, bespectacled man of forty-one with a neat mustache and a carefully groomed conservative Afro haircut — and gave a little laugh. "I was able to express my thanks. I appreciate that honor.

I think it means something. I was born and raised in Hempstead County, and I got my education at the University of Arkansas, at Pine Bluff. I came into Hope to live in nineteen sixty-one, and started teaching here in nineteen sixty-five. I like Hope. It's a cautiously progressive town for the South. I've learned this: as far as achievement is concerned, if a black man really tries to achieve he won't find a lot of resistance — white or black. Oh, you find some. I did. But they finally realize you're trying to better the community. The older whites are usually more supportive than the younger ones. I think that's because they've had time to get rid of a lot of preconceived notions. Another thing, of course, is that the blacks and the whites have always had a more human relationship in the South — in the small-town South. It's easier to hate a man if you don't know him, and here in a little town like Hope, everybody knows everybody else. You can't forget your common humanity if you're standing face to face. There's also something else. Blacks learn better in a small town. Everybody goes to the same school. I don't mean it's easy. I've got three boys, and we talk, and they're always saying the teachers make them prove themselves over and over again. But that's all right. Education is the key. For everybody, but especially — and vitally, right now — for the blacks. Our children have got to learn. I go along with Jesse Jackson: Turn that TV *off*."

✦

A day or two later, I talked with a younger black achiever. He was a senior at the Hope High School, just turned eighteen, named Dwayne Stanley, and he had just been awarded a scholarship to Ouachita Baptist University (coeducational, founded 1885), at Arkadelphia, Arkansas. Stanley, like Young, has a trim, conservative Afro, and he also has much of the same poise and presence. We sat at a table in the school library, and as we talked he tugged gently at a little goatee. "I was really lucky," he told me. "It's a *full* scholarship — it pays for everything but books. I play football and I play baseball and I'm pretty fast in track, but I'm only six feet tall and I only weigh one-seventy-five, so I quit thinking about a career in sports. I'll go into physical education if I have to. But what I really want to do is get into data processing and computer programming. That would mean leaving Hope. The nearest place for that kind of job is down in Texarkana. There's a lot I like about Hope. My daddy is in the Air Force — he's a senior master sergeant in radar — and we've lived in a lot of places: North Carolina, Sacramento, Colorado Springs. I prefer Hope. It's nice and quiet. If I get uptight at night, I can go out for a walk and don't have to worry about anybody bothering me. It's not a city. There's a little bit of racism here, not too much, but things are calming down. I get along with everybody at school. I've been the only black at a white party, and it was okay. Nobody made me feel funny. And we treat the white guys the same way at our parties. The thing is, we all *know* each other. Blacks don't date whites, and whites don't date blacks. This isn't a city in that way. But when it happens, nobody makes a big scene about it. The white guys will take the white girl aside and have a little talk. And we'll do the same."

✦

Troy Buck watched me unwrap a Maalox tablet. "I used to take those things," he said. Buck, a big, hefty man with a smiling country-boy look, teaches vocational agriculture at the high school, and I had dropped in at his office after my talk with Dwayne Stanley. "I could work all day out at the farm and my heartburn never bothered me. But when I had a conference or a speech to make — oh, Lord! I ate those Maaloxes by the handful. Then somebody suggested that I try chewing to-

bacco. I know that sounds funny, but it worked. Maybe it's all
psychological, but it works. I take a chew every morning and
after every meal. I don't think it's the brand I chew. They're
probably all alike. But what I chew is Levi Garrett."

Buck is not, by far, the only man in Hope who chews tobacco. He is merely (as far as I know) the only man who chews
for reasons of health. Sales of chewing tobacco are up throughout the United States, and Hope is an enthusiastic participant in
this curious (sports-generated?) revival. The Safeway Store has
four shelves devoted to chewing tobaccos (Cannon Ball, Work
Horse, Red Horse, Red Man, Beech-Nut, Conwood, Big Duke,
Union Standard, Taylor's Pride, and Days Work as well as Levi
Garrett) and three more devoted to snuffs (Good Luck, Co-
penhagen, Gold River, Silver Creek, Kodiak, Dental Scotch, W.
E. Garrett, Tube Rose, and Devon's Eagle).

◆

Sunday in Hope is a day very largely shaped by Christian faith
and social convention. Hope is not a Sabbatarian town. It is,
however, a churchgoing town, and for all but its two hun-
dred-odd Roman Catholics services usually begin with Sunday
School (classes for both adults and children), at nine-thirty;
followed by Morning Worship, at ten-forty-five; followed by
an afternoon Church Training Program; followed, at seven
o'clock, by Evening Worship. Almost everybody in Hope — old
or young, white or black — attends at least one of these services,
and there are some who attend them all. I chose, on the second
Sunday of my stay, to attend Morning Worship at the First
Baptist Church.

The nave of the First Baptist Church seats six hundred and
fifty people in comfortably cushioned pews, and there is room
for over two hundred more in a balcony. When I arrived and
was shown to a place, the nave looked almost full, and there

were also people in the balcony. Most of the worshippers were
families with one or more (well-behaved) children. It was a
congregation of Sunday suits and Sunday bests. There were no
turtlenecks, no pantsuits, not even, as far as I could tell, any
sports jackets: all the men wore business suits, and all the
women wore dresses. An organ and a piano flanked the pulpit,
and there was a large choir. Dr. Richard Stiltner, the pastor, a
youthful-looking man with an expressive face, wore a dark suit.
After the opening prayer, we sang "O Worship the King," and
after the Invocation and another prayer we sang "Rock of Ages,
Cleft for Me." Dr. Stiltner's sermon was one of a series on the
Ten Commandments. It was entitled "The Sanctity of Life,"
and dealt with the Sixth Commandment. "This commandment
is commonly taken to read, 'Thou shalt not kill,' " he said. "A
more careful rendering of the Hebrew is 'Thou shalt not
murder.' " He said that the Old Testament accepts the right of a
soldier to take a human life in war, and it accepts the right of
society to inflict the death penalty. We sang a final hymn,
"Something for Thee," and received the Benediction. Dr.
Stiltner waited in the vestibule to greet the departing congregation. I saw Hulan White, immaculate in a tan summer suit,
and a dozen other familiar faces. And half an hour later, at the
ritual Sunday dinner in the restaurant at the Quality Inn, I
recognized several of my fellow worshippers. Most of my fellow
diners began their meal with the usual apéritif of the region — a
cup of coffee.

✦

I spent an hour that Sunday afternoon strolling in Rose Hill
Cemetery, on North Hazel Street. Rose Hill is the oldest cemetery in Hope, and like most old cemeteries it has a soothing
worn and weathered beauty. Many of its gravestones are tilted
or sunken, and its paths and drives are shaded by big, whisper-

ing cedars and magnolias, and that afternoon the air was sweet with the scent of wild-plum blossoms. Wandering among the graves, glancing at the names and dates on the stones, I began to notice a melancholy pattern in many of the epitaphs: a stark brevity of life. Annie V. Shelton (1892–1912), dead at twenty. Alfred Forbes (1894–1900), dead at six. Samuel Edwards (1886–1887), aged one year. James Betts (1895–1898), Maude Wainwright (1885–1902), Allen Edward Ruffin (1889–1892), Ruth Agnes Ruffin (1895–1900), Gaines Trotter Ruffin (1900–1905).

The following day, talking to one of Hope's senior physicians, a general practitioner named George Wright, I mentioned those baleful testimonials of a not too distant time. "People forget how it used to be," he told me. "Those were the days before antibiotics, before much immunization. We hardly think about the infectious diseases these days, but they were the killers then. Measles. Whooping cough. Scarlet fever. Diphtheria. Pneumonia — especially pneumonia. It killed everybody, all ages. Now it's an old man's disease. It's what finally puts him out of his misery. We call it the old man's friend. But nothing ever really changes. We still have our big killers. No, I don't mean cancer and heart disease. I mean the truly modern killers. There are two of them. One is appetite. The other is lethargy. They're the great American curse."

✦

"You mean that set of harness?" LaGrone Williams said. We were standing in the cramped and cluttered center aisle of his hardware store, on Elm Street, looking up at a huge, spidery apparition of shiny black leather and shiny steel buckles dangling from the ceiling like a monstrous, overimaginative mobile. "Sure, it's real. And it's new. I'm not in the antiques business. I *sell* harness. I sell two or three sets a year. I also sell horse collars and backbands and hames and cotton plowlines. The workhorse is coming back. It's the energy problem, I reckon. People are getting tired of feeding a horse just to ride. They're making their saddle horse start earning his keep. I call them one-horse farmers. They're not real farmers. They're just folks that have a few acres that they want to put to some use, and they don't want the cost and the bother of machinery. Some of them that don't have a horse are going out and buying themselves an old Missouri mule. A lot of people are looking back to the past. They think there's a lot of progress back there. I'm selling them Georgia plows and new-ground plows — what used to be called sodbusters. And just the other day I sold a man a broadaxe. That's the tool they built the old log cabins with."

✦

I drove out one morning to the Split Hickory Company, a few miles north of town, and spent an hour with the executive vice-president, a big, gentle, balding man named James M. Lockhart, in his aromatic office there. "That's right," he told me. "We're just about the only folks in our line of business. We make canes — stockmen's canes. They're our biggest product. We make around thirty-five hundred per week, and we can sell as many as we make. We sell a lot of them to banks and insurance companies, and they give them away to their good customers. We also make show sticks and sorting poles and shepherds' crooks. There are still shepherds in this country. Show sticks are what the shower uses to make his bull perform for the judges. Look at this stack of orders — Pennsylvania, Kansas, Idaho, Michigan. Heck, we've got customers everywhere. We've got a customer up on Fifth Avenue in New York that sells our canes and shepherds' crooks to men and women that like to walk in Central Park. I reckon a big, stout cane makes them feel easier in their mind about muggers. We sell a lot of sorting poles to circuses. Ringling Brothers is a big account. They use our poles to train their big cats. We're the only folks that make an elephant cane. It's like a stockman's stick, only thicker. We make dowels that a company in Pennsylvania shapes into drumsticks. We don't set out to make dowels — they're a by-product of our canes. Pieces too short for anything else. Ladder rungs are another by-product, and so are hickory chips for barbecues. We sell our sawdust to garages and body shops to soak up their oil. My sons and I — they're working out in the shop — we carry home the discarded chunks of hickory logs for firewood. The only thing we haven't been able to salvage is the knot. My oldest boy is working on that."

✦

Rogers — Pod Rogers, the circulation director of the *Star* — handed me a copy of the *Guinness Book of World Records*. It was opened to page 118, and a paragraph halfway down the page was marked. It read, "Largest melons: A watermelon weighing 200 lbs. was reported in Apr. 1980. The growers were Ivan and Lloyd Bright, of Hope, Ark." Rogers is a beaming, twinkling, foot-tapping man in his middle fifties, and he watched me read, beaming and twinkling and tapping his foot. "Didn't know that, did you?" he said. "Well, we've been growing champion watermelons here for years. This is the watermelon capital of the world. A man named Gibson had a drugstore back in the twenties, and he started offering a cash prize for the biggest melon grown here every year. That was the beginning of our annual Watermelon Festival. It faded for a number of years, but I revived it in nineteen seventy-seven. The champion melon up to the Brights' two-hundred-pounder was grown back in nineteen thirty-nine and weighed one hundred and ninety-five pounds. Everybody was shooting at that mark for forty years. Okay. Now, then. I've been talking to Ivan Bright, and he's

going to be home this morning, and I'm going to carry you out
to his place to meet him. What do you drink? Coke? Dr Pepper?
Or what? Help yourself from that machine, and let's get going."

There was a bumper sticker on Rogers's car. It showed a
red-and-green slice of watermelon and read, "Hope, Arkansas,
a Slice of the Good Life." The car was comfortably air-conditioned, and there was a pleasant murmur of music, and the
dashboard was equipped at either end with ringed holders for
Rogers's Coke and my Dr Pepper. "My interest in the festival is
simply this," Rogers told me. "I figure that what's good for
Hope is good for the *Star*. The festival is three days in the last
week in August. That's harvest time for melons. The climax is
the watermelon-weighing on our certified scales in the Coliseum, out at Fair Park, but there's more to it than that. There's
dancing in the streets to four different styles of music, and we
have a watermelon-eating contest. Our big melons are as good
to eat as they're big. And a watermelon-seed-spitting contest
and a cow-chip-throwing contest and a sack race and arm-
wrestling — something for everybody. People ask me what it
takes to grow a big melon. I say it takes the right seed, the right
soil, the right climate, the know-how, and they've got to live in
Hope, Arkansas. Maybe you didn't know this — the watermelon is a desert fruit. It was brought here from Africa back in
the old slavery times. But all I really care about is putting Hope,
Arkansas, on the map. That white house up yonder — that's the
Bright place. Ivan is Lloyd's daddy. Lloyd teaches up at Arkadelphia, but he was right here on the scene when they grew
that world-famous melon." We pulled into the driveway.
Rogers rolled down his window and yelled, "*Ivan* — you've got
company!"

The front door opened, and Bright came out. He is a thin,
weathered man with a bony face and a long, nutcracker jaw. He

was wearing a little green hat. Rogers introduced us, and he gave me a limp country handshake, and the three of us leaned against the side of the car. Bright pointed across a cow pasture to the slope of a distant hill. That was the site of his 1979 watermelon patch. "We move the patch every year," he told me. "Watermelon diseases easy. You want to keep a jump ahead. You need a well-drained sandy loam for melons, which I've got here, and you need the right kind of seed. What Lloyd and I used was a cross between a Cobb Gem and a Carolina Cross. Planting time is the last of April. We plant two seeds to a hill — two hundred hills, and fifteen feet between the hills. Then you watch the vines develop, and you thin out all but the best. Then you watch the melons come along. You look for the best-looking — the most likely to take the right shape. You water each vine only every three days. You don't want standing water. And you don't water in the morning or it'll steam under the sun and kill it. I'm talking about late August, when the temperature is over a hundred all the time. Well, that August in nineteen seventy-nine, Lloyd and I we had a feeling we might get a good melon. We had our eye on one. When it hit a hundred pounds, we knew it was going to be big. We also had another that looked pretty good, but darned if it didn't stop growing at one eighty-three. But this one just kept growing. The festival began, and the deadline for melons was on Sunday, August twenty-sixth. The day before, on Saturday, August twenty-fifth, we rigged the melon up on an old set of balance-type cotton scales. We used a gunnysack, and we handled it very careful. It weighed one ninety-eight and a half. Lloyd decided to lay out in the patch beside it all night. He wanted to guarantee that nothing went wrong at the last minute. At midnight, he went over with his flashlight, and it was still one ninety-eight and a half. I got up just after sunrise and went out to the patch. It was still the same. But melons don't grow a heck of a lot at night. So Lloyd and I we waited there. The sun came up, and the scale began to stir a little. That melon was still growing. We watched it go up and up, and when it hit an even two hundred, we pulled it. I think it would surely have gone higher, but we were late with our entry, so we pulled it. I think it might have gone up five more pounds. But we pulled it and got it down to the Coliseum and on the official scales. And they said we had the winner — the all-time winner. We had the biggest watermelon anybody ever grew. Lloyd and I we felt right good about it. Especially when a fellow from Magnolia offered us a hundred dollars for a dozen seeds from the champion."

✦

The entrance to the Hope *Star* offices is a vestibule, and on one of my visits to Pod Rogers I reached it a step ahead of a young woman. I opened the outer door and held it for her to pass. She thanked me and went through and then held open the inner door for me. I went through, and thanked her in turn.

"That's okay," she said. "An eye for an eye."

✦

The masthead of the *Star* includes an outline map of Hempstead County superimposed on a drawing of a knife. An accompanying legend reads, "Home of the Bowie Knife." The specific birthplace of the Bowie knife (to those who accept its Hempstead County origin) is a hamlet called Washington, some ten miles northwest of Hope. Washington was the original seat of Hempstead County, and during the Civil War, when the Union forces occupied Little Rock, it became the seat of the refugee Confederate government of Arkansas. It is now very largely the Old Washington Historic State Park, and one of its places of historic interest (along with the Old Courthouse, the Old Methodist Church, and the Old Tavern Inn) is the Gun

Museum, which houses an important collection of antique firearms and Bowie knives. "One thing is certain," Gene Redmond, the curator, told me. "Jim Bowie spent time here. Washington was the gateway to the old Chihuahua Trail. And he had a knife made here in eighteen thirty-one by a blacksmith named Jim Black. Those knives in that case there are modern Bowie knives. They're interpretations by modern craftsmen. You can see how they vary in length — from eight or ten inches to up to a foot and a half. We've got several very good knife-makers in this area. Genuine Bowie knives are rare — or, anyway, hard to authenticate. Bowie lost his, of course, when he died that day in eighteen thirty-six at the Alamo. It's uncertain just how the Bowie knife came about. Black was an expert knifemaker, and he had already made a famous knife — a long, pointed dagger — that they called the Arkansas Toothpick. The distinctive things about the Bowie knife as Bowie and Black worked it out were its guard and the curved blade that turned back on top to form a clip, or scimitar, end. The Bowie knife was not a hunting knife. It was a fighting knife — guns were too unreliable to fight with in those days. It was a man-killer. The guard was bent forward to face the blade and catch your opponent's thrust. And the sharpened upper blade was so when you stabbed your man you could give your knife an upward pull and rip his stomach out. Davy Crockett is supposed to have said that Bowie's knife was so ferocious-looking it made you puke just to look at it. There's another thing about Jim Bowie. He may have been a good knife fighter, and he probably was. He survived a lot of knife fights. But he was also a liar and a braggart and a crook. He was an all-around bastard."

✦

"I guess you could call it a Bowie knife," Edward Hill told me. "A lot of people do. But what *I* call it is a Hill knife." Hill, a retired blacksmith, is one of the several local expert knife-makers mentioned by Gene Redmond. I had driven out to see him at his home, in the crossroads village of Saratoga, just to the west of Hempstead County, and he was showing me some of his knives. "I mean I styled it and I made it," he said. "I start with a piece of gang-saw steel. Those old saw blades come about five feet long and five inches wide and about an eighth of an inch thick. I cut them down to the general size I want. For a knife like you've got there in your hand, where I want a five-inch blade, I'll cut out a length of nine and a half inches. Four and a half is for the handle. Then I cut it to shape and finish off the blade with emery paper. But all that grinding and papering will have taken out the temper. So I got to put it back. I've got a little gas forge out in my shop. Tempering is heating the steel, then cooling it off — quenching it — quick. Steel when you heat it goes through different color stages. They call them early blue, light blue, straw, and cherry red. Some fellows like to take it all the way to cherry red. I don't. I only take it to light blue. I think cherry red makes your steel brittle, and your edge is likely to chip. I only temper the blade, of course. If the handle was tempered, I'd have a handle too hard to drill through for fixing on the grip. I've got a lot of different kinds of grip. I've got a hunter friend who keeps me supplied with deer horn and elk horn, and when I want a wooden grip I'll go out and cut it for myself. I use oak sometimes, and bois d'arc, which is the hardest wood of all and just won't rot, and black walnut. That knife you have there has a walnut grip. That wavy stuff in walnut, what they call the grain, makes it real pretty when you dress it down. The trouble is, black walnut is getting scarce. I don't know why, but the tree is dying out. There are guys going around looking for old walnut stumps to buy and dig up, roots and all, and sell to the cabinetmakers for a good price.

But we were talking about the Bowie knife. That day is over. They don't fight with knives anymore, they fight with guns. So my knife isn't a fighting knife. I sell my knives to hunters who want a good knife for skinning. I go to those arts-and-crafts fairs and show my knives, and I've got customers all over — Georgia, Texas, Missouri, Louisiana. Some of them try to tell me how they want it made. I'll listen and be reasonable, but I generally manage to get my mark on it, my style."

✦

Walking along West Second Street one afternoon, I glanced in the window at Herbert Burns, Inc., and saw Hulan White standing up near the front of his store with two neckties draped over his arm and tying another around the neck of an elderly man. The man was standing stiffly at attention and staring straight ahead. I watched White finish tying the necktie, then loosen the noose and slip it off over the old man's head. Then he tied one of the other ties and slipped it off and went to work tying the third. I went in the store and waited while White wrapped up the three ready-tied ties and the old man paid and left. White came over to me, smiling a little smile. "That's one of our special services," he said. "A lot of stores in towns like this do the same. We have quite a few customers who don't know how to tie a necktie. They're young men, old men, and middle-aged. Black and white. What they are is men who don't wear a necktie every day — maybe only to church on Sunday, or to a wedding or a funeral — and they just never got around to learning how to tie a four-in-hand knot."

✦

It was during my stay in Hope that Arkansas became the first state to enact into law the so-called creation-science proposition, which requires a public school that teaches the theory of biological evolution to teach a companion course presenting the origin of man as recounted in the Book of Genesis. Among the many state legislators who voted for the measure was the representative of the Twentieth District, which includes Hempstead County — a handsome, bright-eyed, twenty-nine-year-old law student named Keith Wood. Wood was born and raised and lives in Hope, and I talked with him one afternoon in his little book-lined office on the fourth floor of the Hempstead County Courthouse. He offered me a Coke from a machine, took one for himself, pushed aside a copy of *The American Rifleman,* and smiled at me across his desk. "You bet I voted for SB 482," he told me. "And I'm proud I did. I've only been married a year, and I don't have any children yet myself, but when I do I want them to have an opportunity to learn another side to the question of how man appeared on earth. Some people say that SB 482 will mean teaching religion in the schools. No, sir. If you're giving the kids an option, you're not teaching religion. What you're teaching them is to use their own minds and think for themselves. They talk about the Missing Link in evolution. I say, what's the problem? If you take the Bible approach, you won't find any so-called Missing Link — because there isn't any. Man was created man. God created certain levels of animals and plants and all, and everything evolved from that, rather than out of some molecule or cell or something. I believe that. I face all the issues. Take Prohibition, for example. I stand for that. Hempstead County is dry, and I like it that way. I intend to do all I can to keep it dry. I'm not a drinking man, and I want my children to be the same. I want them to grow up straight."

✦

"Fifth Avenue was really neat," Sandra Yocom told me. "I never saw anything like it before." Miss Yocom, a pretty girl of seventeen with wide-set green eyes and a luxuriance of soft, curling brown hair, was one of a group of Hope High School juniors and seniors who spent three days in New York in mid-March on a visit arranged by the school. "I did get kind of scared sometimes," she said. "Everybody was always saying hang on to your purse. But the whole trip was neat. We drove up to Little Rock and flew from there to St. Louis and then on to New York. I'd never been in a 727 before, and that made me kind of edgy for a while. We stayed at the Piccadilly Hotel, on West Forty-fifth Street, so we were close to Fifth Avenue. My three best girl friends and I did a lot of shopping and looking around. We were walking on Fifth one day in broad daylight, and this dirty-looking man pointed his finger at us and said, 'I'm going to eat your brains.' We just burst out laughing. Another time, we saw a crazy man standing there on the street talking to a trash can. New York is certainly different. I bought a pair of pants at Saks. That's a neat store. So is Macy's. Dillard's in Texarkana was the biggest store I'd seen before — but, my Lord! Saks had *five* rows of cosmetics and perfumes. We saw *A Chorus Line*. It was my first play, and it was really great. It was beautiful — all those dances and costumes. I just loved it. Another thing I liked about New York was the water. I thought it tasted *so* good. I really thought it was as good as our water here in Hope. We went down to the World Trade Center one day to see the view from the top — from the one-hundred-and-seventh floor. On the way up in the elevator, when we came to the seventy-eighth floor there was a sound like a tornado. I asked a man what *that* was. He said it was the wind. He said that right about where we were the building swayed as much as three feet. I said in my country-hick voice, 'Are you kidding me?' I mean, I just could *not* believe it. When we got to the top and looked out, all you could see as far as you could see was New York City. It was just New York City spread out as far as you could see. That really impressed me. I just had trouble comprehending it. We ate dinner at the Windows on the World restaurant. The others all ordered shrimp cocktails to start with and then either steak or chicken. But I wanted to branch out. Why should I eat the same kind of food I can eat at home? So I started out with a salmon paté. Then I had sea trout. It came with a little, bitty black fish on top with its little, bitty eyes looking up at me. It had a saffron-and-tomato sauce. I didn't much like that sauce. I guess I'm a finicky eater. I like my catfish down here better. But, good Lord, you have to be willing to try new things. So I'm glad I did what I did. One night, we went to the Radio City Music Hall, my three friends and me, and when we came out we walked up the street and came around a corner — and there was St. Patrick's Cathedral! I mean, there was this beautiful church in the middle of all that tall concrete. Our mouths just dropped open. It was really neat. I made one mistake. I should never have worn my cowboy boots. My legs began to hurt with all that walking. We went to the Stage Door Deli, and a man there, a waiter, showed us where Jimmy Carter had sat. The only thing I missed in New York was Dr Pepper. They just didn't seem to know about Dr Pepper anywhere. So on the way home, when we stopped for gas at Arkadelphia I jumped out and had a great big Dr Pepper."